THE
COOPER-HEWITT
DYNASTY OF NEW YORK

POLLY GUÉRIN

Charleston | London

THE
History
PRESS

Published by The History Press
Charleston, SC 29403
www.historypress.net

Copyright © 2012 by Polly Guérin
All rights reserved

First published 2012

Manufactured in the United States

ISBN 978.1.60949.860.3

Library of Congress CIP data applied for.

For my father, George Guérin.

Contents

Author's Note

The *Cooper-Hewitt Dynasty of New York* has been a work in progress for several years. During that time, I was a professor at the Fashion Institute of Technology in New York City. On a study trip, I took one of my classes to visit the Smithsonian, Cooper-Hewitt National Design Museum. I was fascinated by the fact that Peter Cooper's granddaughters—Sarah Cooper Hewitt, Eleanor Garnier Hewitt and Amy Hewitt Green—were credited as the founders of the museum. So, being the history sleuth that I am, I inquired in the museum's gift store if there was a book about these women and their connection to Peter Cooper, the great American industrialist, and his free college, The Cooper Union.

"No, we do not have a book like that in stock," the sales clerk informed me. "That's so disappointing," I replied. The salesperson looked at me over his bifocal glasses and said, "Why don't you write one yourself?"

And that, dear readers, is how it came about that I began my research several years ago to write about the Cooper-Hewitt dynasty of New York. The book is divided into three sections because one cannot tell the story of these important Knickerbocker families without starting with Peter Cooper, the grand patriarch of the clan, a masterful inventor, industrialist and philanthropist affectionately referred to as the "first citizen of Old New York." He was a prolific entrepreneur and is best known as the founder of his free college, The Cooper Union for the Advancement of Science & Art, where he had always planned to have a museum for the benefit of the students and inquiring public.

The Hewitt sisters' father, Abram Stevens Hewitt (designated as "America's foremost private citizen") shares the platform of dignitaries in this saga. Hewitt was also a self-made man, and like Peter Cooper, he was an astute businessman, politician, ironmaster and philanthropist. He came into the Cooper circle by marrying Cooper's only daughter, Sarah Amelia. Being of French descent, Hewitt had innate cultural sensitivity that he passed on to the young Hewitt sisters, encouraging as he did their interest in the decorative arts. In keeping with dynastic tradition, he served as president of The Cooper Union and fully endorsed The Cooper Union museum project and supported its development.

The Hewitt sisters—Amy, Sarah and Eleanor—were remarkable women for their time, and while they could have remained society belles, their métier was the decorative arts. They chose careers as the curatrixes of The Cooper Union Museum for the Arts of Decoration. Although the three sisters were involved with the museum project from the start, Amy married Dr. James Olive Green and from then on had limited involvement. Sarah and Eleanor, therefore, took over the formidable task and spent their lifetime and their fortune on procuring works for their museum, with a focus on the decorative arts.

Ringwood Manor, the Cooper-Hewitt country estate, figures importantly in the collective lives of the Cooper-Hewitt dynasty. It has a rich historical background supplying iron ore for ammunition and guns going back to the American Revolution. Iron ore also made the Cooper-Hewitts rich entrepreneurs and celebrated ironmasters of the nineteenth century. In the 1850s, with the decline of industrial activity, Ringwood became a popular country retreat, and the Cooper-Hewitts, who were among America's social elite, took up residence year round at Ringwood Manor.

The legacy of the Cooper-Hewitt dynasty in New York reaches far and wide and enriches the lives of people today through the Hewitt sisters' Cooper Union Museum for the Arts of Decoration, which was officially launched in 1897. The Hewitt sisters' museum was renamed in 1994 as the Smithsonian, Cooper-Hewitt National Design Museum. It continues the tradition set by the Hewitt sisters and is the only museum in the nation devoted exclusively to historic and contemporary design. It heightens the awareness of design and the decorative arts through its groundbreaking exhibitions and educational programs.

Acknowledgements

I wish to extend my gratitude to all the curators and librarians at the research centers, museums and libraries I used, without whom writing this book would have been impossible. With special thanks, I recognize the generous input of Sue Shutte, resource interpretative specialist, Ringwood Manor, Ringwood State Park, New Jersey, for her consummate knowledge of the Hewitt family.

The personal recollections of the Hewitt family by Mrs. Robert Hewitt Stanwood provided insight about Abram Steven Hewitt's brothers, who worked in the Cooper-Hewitt iron industry and glue business. Her collection of gowns and other clothing once owned by the Hewitt sisters substantiates her role as the keeper of historical Hewitt family data.

I would also like to extend my gratitude to Elbertus Prol, curator (retired), Ringwood Manor, Ringwood State Park. His intimate knowledge of Ringwood Manor and the Hewitt family who resided there authenticated historical facts.

I particularly want to mention the late Melanie James, the library assistant at the General Society Library of the Mechanics & Tradesman of the City of New York, who opened the library's historical stacks to many research books, including Allan Nevins's book, *Abram S. Hewitt with Some Account of Peter Cooper*. It was interesting to discover that Peter Cooper was an early member of the General Society of Mechanics & Tradesmen, to which he was admitted as a member in 1837, listed as a "Glue Maker," a tradesman term that Cooper preferred.

Chris Sonne, Tuxedo Park town historian, met me at the Tuxedo Park Library to open up the Tuxedo Club membership books and maps of the Tuxedo Park/Ringwood area. The Ringwood Public Library's extensive collection of Louis Preston West's "I Remember Ringwood" series provided Mr. West's personal recollections of living and working on the Ringwood estate and his relationship with the Hewitt family.

The Cooper Union Library archives were a rich source of research and an opportunity to view newspaper accounts of the family's society weddings, the Ladies Amateur Orchestra and a collection of personal scrapbooks and artifacts.

The Hewitt sisters' little leather travel diaries, housed in the Cooper-Hewitt National Design Museum Library, provided an intimate view of the sisters' succinct notations about the historic sites they visited during their European trips.

I also wish to thank Lorraine Allen, archivist, All Souls Church, New York City, for details of Peter Cooper's life and of his friendship with Dr. Henry Whitney Bellows. Nathan C. Walker's article from the biography of Peter Cooper for the Unitarian Universalist Historical Society (UUHS) provided a detailed account of Peter Cooper's life.

I would be remiss if I did not mention the Huguenot Society of America, which substantiated the genealogy on the Hewitt family tree and the surname change from "Garnier" to "Gurnee" as recorded in the French Church.

My friend Jean Ward-Greenway introduced me to Ringwood Manor at a spring tea several years ago and thus fueled my interest in the Cooper-Hewitts' country retreat.

Foremost in the rank of recognition, this book would not have been possible without references to Edward Ringwood Hewitt's intimate remembrances of his family, as well as Eleanor Garnier Hewitt's historical account in *The Making of a Modern Museum*.

I have met many wonderful people during my research who were all enthusiastic about the book. However, if I have neglected to mention anyone else specifically, I do sincerely apologize for that oversight.

Introduction

This work introduces the lives of the patriarchs of the Cooper-Hewitt families, who contributed exponentially to the historical development of the Dutch settlement that became New York. The history of the dynasty spans more than one hundred years from 1791, when the legendary patriarch Peter Cooper was born, until 1903, when his son-in-law, Abram Stevens Hewitt, died. The dynasty stretched further into the 1930s with the death of the last surviving Hewitt daughter, Sarah, in 1930 and Hewitt son, Erskine, in 1938. The Cooper-Hewitts' progeny reach far and wide, with descendants of the clan who, like their forebearers, are engaged in many branches of industry, politics and philanthropy.

Peter Cooper was the quintessential mechanic, glue manufacturer, inventor, ironmaster and philanthropist, and New Yorkers regarded their oldest citizen as a living treasure. Throughout his long life, Cooper was sincerely grateful for the many opportunities that America had given him and was fervently patriotic, as was his son-in-law, Abram Stevens Hewitt. In his time, Cooper inspired the charitable acts and civic responsibilities of other tycoons, including Andrew Carnegie, George Peabody, Matthew Vassar and Ezra Cornell. While Peter Cooper founded The Cooper Union for the Advancement of Science and Art, it was Abram Stevens Hewitt who was the institute's administrator and president.

Like Cooper, Abram Stevens Hewitt, the second patriarch, was a successful businessman, ironmaster and politician. Hewitt's character, interests and achievements were so markedly similar to Cooper's that one

Sarah Amelia Hewitt. *Courtesy of The Cooper Union.*

might consider that the two men were soul mates. Hewitt, like Cooper, was a man of strong moral fiber and was heavily involved in inventions and industrialization. A lawyer by training, Abram Stevens Hewitt distinguished himself in politics and was a member of the United States Congress from 1874 to 1886, and he was one-term mayor of New York City from 1887 to 1888.

When Hewitt married Peter Cooper's daughter Sarah Amelia, the fate of these two families was combined into one household. The Hewitts had six children, and they all lived together with Peter Cooper in his stately home in New York City, with visits taking place at their Ringwood Manor estate in Ringwood, New Jersey, during most of the summer months and often in the winter.

Ringwood itself is steeped in historical lore, and from its mines has come iron for every war of the United States from the Revolution War right up to World War I. Ringwood was an important part of the development of the iron industry in this country and was a source of the Cooper-Hewitt fortune.

Throughout their lifetime, Peter Cooper and Abram Stevens Hewitt left their indelible imprints on New York in politics, business, education and philanthropy. Cooper was the first rich man to preach year after year that wealth is a trust, carrying paramount duties and obligations. In his lifetime, his philosophy influenced other wealthy men to take up the gauntlet of philanthropy to establish libraries, schools and hospitals.

This is a sprawling saga, from rags to riches, starting with Peter Cooper and continuing with Abram Stevens Hewitt, who fulfilled the great man's legacy, and finally the Hewitt sisters. The sisters' extraordinary lives as curatrixes, their wealth and their connections, made possible The Cooper Union Museum for the Arts of Decoration, which became the Smithsonian, Cooper-Hewitt National Design Museum.

PART I

Peter Cooper

First Citizen of Old New York

Peter Cooper came from Dutch-American ancestors distinguished for their unwavering devotion to the cause of American independence.

On the paternal side of Cooper's family tree, the earliest account of his Dutch heritage links back to Peter Cooper's great-great-grandfather, Abraham Cooper, who emigrated from the Netherlands and settled in 1662 at Fishkill-on-Hudson. In 1749, Peter's grandfather, Obadiah Cooper II, married Esther Terbos and permanently settled in Dutchess County, where Esther and Obadiah's son, John Cooper, was born.

When the Revolutionary War began, John Cooper was among the first to enlist in the fight to free the colonies from British rule, serving as a sergeant in the regiment of local Fishkill minutemen. He served for four years at West Point.

GENERAL JOHN CAMPBELL

In the early years of the country's struggle for independence, Deputy Quartermaster General John Campbell, Peter Cooper's maternal grandfather, was a man of considerable wealth and sacrificed a large

PETER COOPER FAMILY TREE

GRANDPARENTS

Obadiah Cooper II (1720–1776)

BORN: Albany, New York

Dutch ancestry

Married 1749 to Esther Terbos
(1726–1789)

General John Campbell (1744–1807)

BORN: New York City

Served in the Continental army

Married 1761 to Sarah Oakley
(1745–unknown)

Son of Obadiah and Esther

• John O. Cooper

Daughter of John and Sarah

• Margaret Campbell

PARENTS

John O. Cooper (1755–1838)

BORN: Fishkill, New York

Served in the Continental army

Margaret Campbell (1762–1841)

BORN: New York City

John and Margaret Cooper married in 1779 and had seven children. Their fifth child was son Peter Cooper.

Sarah Bedell's parents (Huguenot ancestry)
    Benjamin Bedell (1753–1840) married Mary Raynor (1760–1823)
    DAUGHTER: Sarah Raynor Bedell

Peter Cooper (1791–1883)

BORN: New York City

Dutch/American ancestry

FOUNDER: The Cooper Union

Sarah Raynor Bedell (1793–1869)

BORN: Hempstead, Long Island

Huguenot ancestry

Peter and Sarah Cooper married in 1813 and had six children, two of whom (*) survived to adulthood.

John Cooper (1814–1820)
Benjamin Cooper (1815–1819)
Sarah Cooper (1820–1824)
Peter Cooper (1822–1824)
Edward Cooper (1824–1905)*
Sarah Amelia Cooper (1830–1912)*

Edward Cooper (1824–1905) and Cornelia Redmond (1828–1873) married in 1887 and had two children. Edward served as mayor of New York from 1879 to 1880.

Edith Cooper (1854–1916)
Peter Cooper (1860–unknown)

Edith Cooper (1854–1916) and Lloyd Stephens Bryce (1851–1917) married in 1879 and had three children. Bryce served as U.S. Representative from New York from 1887 to 1889.

Edith Clare Bryce (1880–1960)
Cornelia "Leila" Bryce (1881–1960)
Peter Cooper Bryce (1889–1964)

Sarah Amelia Cooper (1830–1912), Peter Cooper's daughter, and Abram Stevens Hewitt (1822–1903) married in 1855. Hewitt served as mayor of New York from 1887 to 1888.

fortune in the cause of his country's freedom. In the end, however, Campbell had nothing but a large quantity of worthless Continental money as an acknowledgement. Peter Cooper, recalling this historical fact, often laughed at this "paper payment" but admitted that "it was precious stuff, after all, for it was an essential means of our gaining our Independence."

A ROMANTIC EPISODE

During his sojourn under General Campbell's command, Sergeant Cooper was assigned to look after the general's horses while being supervised by the general's seventeen-year-old daughter, Margaret Campbell. Thrown into such intimacy, a romance was destined to happen, and in 1779, during one musical evening, the young couple simply walked off and got married.

It was obviously an outrageous thing for a sergeant to do, and especially without parental consent. You can imagine General Campbell's outrage—he promptly ordered that Sergeant Cooper be shot. That order was commuted to thirty days in the guardhouse. Fortunately, he served only one day, and then he was pardoned on petition from his young wife, Margaret.

The union of John Cooper and Margaret Campbell may have started out like a romance novel, but it would soon turn to the reality of raising and providing for a large family of seven children. Out of this large ménage, John and Margaret's fifth child, Peter Cooper, was destined to become the renowned industrialist, inventor and philanthropist.

PETER COOPER: A MECHANIC OF NEW YORK

America had always been a land of opportunity and held unprecedented promise to daring speculators and inventive entrepreneurs. By the 1850s, Peter Cooper was a prosperous industrialist, and he stands prominently among those inventors who contributed to the industrialization of this country.

He had earned the affection and admiration of the old New Yorkers, who revered Cooper as the city's most prominent father figure. Although

Peter Cooper

Peter Cooper. *Courtesy of the Library of Congress.*

he prospered throughout his long life, and despite his fame and fortune, he insisted on introducing himself simply as "a mechanic of New York."

He was known and respected by the poor and rich alike, who easily recognized the old man walking around town, which he preferred for the sake of economy. He dressed simply, and his austere appearance and legendary frugality were known by almost everyone in old New York. He was of middle stature, but his most recognizable features were his silver locks and beard, which framed his benevolent and venerable face. When the rare occasion required it, Cooper commonly drove about in an old-fashioned one-horse chaise drawn by a steady mare, which gave the onlooker the impression that it belonged to some wealthy farmer or retired tradesman rather than a millionaire.

Throughout his life, however, he made prudent investments, and his entrepreneurial ventures were varied and opportunistic in nature. His success in business was attributed to a faculty for acquiring businesses that had been abandoned by other people, and through perseverance and hard work, he made them succeed.

In order to appreciate how Peter Cooper became the "first citizen of Old New York" and established Cooper Union, it is important to take into account his background and the characteristics that gave him unique traits and opportunity.

PETER COOPER'S EARLY YEARS

Peter Cooper was born unceremoniously in New York City on February 12, 1791, in his father's combination house and hatter's shop on Little Dock Street, now Water Street in lower Manhattan—a spot lined with skyscrapers today. A devout Methodist, John Cooper had strong Christian values and belief in the destiny of his children. His son was given the name Peter, after the great apostle, because his father devoutly believed that he "should come to something." However, Peter Cooper's childhood was one of toil, and disadvantages began early in life. "I have never had any time to get an education," Cooper once almost pathetically remarked, "and all that I know I have had to pick up as I went along."

Lack of a formal education did not prevent Peter from enriching his life. His short ration of books made him anxious to learn, and one of his favorite books was the Bible, which he read and reread. One cannot say with certainty that being poor thwarted his ambition in any negative way. To the contrary, he saw endless opportunity for the future in the young republic, where a man with ideas and the willingness to work hard could succeed if he took the initiative.

In a printed interview housed in The Cooper Union Library archives of 1887, Peter Cooper recalled the circumstance of hardship that his mother, Margaret Campbell, endured: "My mother was an excellent woman, and did the best she could with a large family, narrow circumstances, and a changing home." Peter was always tinkering and began inventing early in adolescence, when he devised a machine for washing clothes to aid his mother's domestic chores.

AN ITINERANT LIFESTYLE

In all of John Cooper's businesses, he was aided by his son Peter, who wrote in his memoir, "My father followed the business of a hatter and the first I

Peter Cooper

Peter Cooper Memorial, New York. *Courtesy of the Library of Congress.*

Another view of the Peter Cooper Memorial. *Courtesy of the Library of Congress.*

remember was being utilized in this business by being set to pull the hair out of rabbit skins, when my head was just barely above the table. I remained in this business until I could make every part of a hat."

Eventually, Peter's father fell out of favor with New York City, and he became enamored of country life and moved the family to Peekskill, New York, where he built a store and became a country grocer. His father may have offered his son Peter an inspiring model of moral behavior, but John Cooper's method of doing business was a different story. He helped his Methodist brothers build a chapel and, forgetting that hospitality could only be supported by a small fortune, John made his house a home for traveling clergy and gave them carte blanche at his grocery store. One might say that "the clergy ate up the profits of the store."

Pursuing other avenues of enterprise, John commenced yet more businesses in Catskill and Newburgh as a brewer and again as a hatter. Peter recalled, "In these business I continued to work with my father until I was seventeen, at which time I left Newburgh and went to New York City to enter the coach making business."

THE APPRENTICE

In Peter Cooper's day, the building of coaches was a great trade, and the work was done by small concerns, where the proprietors and their apprentices would turn out three or four coaches per year. Peter entered as an apprentice to New York coach maker John Woodward of the firm Burtis & Woodward, with which he remained for four years until he had thoroughly learned the business. In his memoir, he recalled, "During my apprenticeship I received twenty-five dollars a year and board for my services and to this sum I added to my small wages by working at ornamental coach carving and sold my handiwork to Woodward and other coachbuilders. My grandmother gave me the use of a room in one of her rear buildings on Broadway, where I spent most of my time in nightly work."

A consummate craftsman at heart, Peter was focused on improving himself and his station in life and remained glued to the grindstone. The youthful inventor once remarked, "During my apprenticeship I made for my employer a machine for mortising the carriage wheel hubs, which proved very profitable to him, and was, perhaps, the first of its kind used in this country." In 1879, Peter Cooper wrote, "That method is still mortising all hubs in the country."

Although Woodward offered to set Cooper up in business, he refused the loan. Cooper reflected, "I always had a horror of being burdened with debt, and having no capital of my own, I declined his kind offer." In so doing, Cooper moved on to explore other business opportunities.

PETER COOPER MARRIES SARAH BEDELL

In 1810, around this time of business indecision, Peter visited his brother Thomas in Hempstead, Long Island, where he was persuaded to work for a man making machines for shearing the nap from cloth. Cooper worked at this business for three years, and with the modest prosperity he had acquired, he began to think of marriage. Into his life entered a young, commonsense woman, Sarah Bedell, of Huguenot ancestry. They were married on December 18, 1813, when Cooper was twenty-two years old and his wife was in her twentieth year, in her parents' home in that Long Island community.

Mrs. Peter Cooper (Sarah Bedell Cooper). *Courtesy of Cooper-Hewitt, National Design Museum, Smithsonian Institution / Art Resource, New York Cooper-Hewitt, National Design Museum, New York City, New York, United States.*

The young couple soon began a family, but infant mortality was a paramount occurrence in those days. They had six children, but sadly four died in childhood. Two lived to adulthood, Edward Cooper and Sarah Amelia, the latter of whom throughout her life was called by her second name, Amelia.

Peter Cooper seemed genuinely kind and indulgent in his domestic life. Always the inventor at heart, he took inspiration from parenting duties. "In early life, when I was first married, I found it necessary to rock the cradle, while my wife prepared our frugal meals. This was not always convenient in my busy life, and I conceived the idea of making a musical cradle that would be made to rock by a mechanism. I did so, and enlarging upon my first idea, I arranged the mechanism for keeping off the flies, and playing a music-box for the amusement of the baby! This cradle was bought from me afterwards, by a delighted peddler, who gave his 'whole stock in trade' for the exchange and privilege of selling the patent in the State of Connecticut."

Cooper was always reinventing or improving machinery and devices for industry, but he vowed that he would never work for another person. Cooper proudly remarked, "I saved enough in the end to buy the right of the State of New York for a machine for shearing cloth, and I commenced the manufacture of these machines on my own account." Then the second war for independence broke out in 1812, cutting off trade with England and enabling Cooper to meet the greater demand of the American weavers and sell his shearing machines as fast as he could make them. He later sold the rights to the shearing machines to Matthew Vassar of Poughkeepsie, New York, and that was the start of his fortune.

COOPER'S VIEW ON DEBT

Peter was very much elated by the success of the sale, and with about $500 garnered from the business, which he considered fine good fortune, he returned to Newburgh to visit his father. His elation was soon deflated, as Peter found the family in dire circumstances, and with the money he had just received from the sale of his machines, he paid off the most pressing of his father's debts. Sadly, in so doing, it left him barely the means to purchase materials to commence the making of new machines.

In 1871, he addressed the subject of debt to The Cooper Union graduates: "I observed that most of the shipwrecks in life were due to debts hastily contracted, and out of proportion to the means of the debtor, and hence I always avoided debt, and endeavored to keep some ready money on hand to avail of a favorable opportunity for its profitable use."

Financial setbacks did not impede his crafty talent for invention; one of his creations inspired the first lawnmower, which had a serendipitous incarnation. "It is worthwhile to mention here that the principle and method of my machine for shearing cloth was precisely the one now used so largely in mowing and reaping machines. This was so obvious that a gentleman seeing my machine at work suggested that a similar machine might be made for mowing grass, and asked me to make a model for this purpose. This was operated for the purpose of cutting the grass in his yard, and it proved entirely successful, long before any machine for mowing had been invented or patented by others."

THE GLUE BUSINESS

The modest foundation of Peter's fortune was gained by the manufacture of glue and his ironworks. Throughout his lifetime, he showed a Yankee talent for undertaking different speculations, as well as great shrewdness and prudence in conducting them. His friend John Vreeland said to him one day, "Why don't you buy that glue factory? It has been mismanaged, but you are the man to make it a success." Cooper looked at the factory and saw its possibilities and access to the raw materials from the nearby slaughterhouses. With what he had made by building machines and in the grocery business in 1821, thirty-year-old Peter purchased the glue factory, buying cheap for a modest $2,000. He acquired its stock and buildings on a lease of twenty-one years for three acres of ground on Sunfish Pond, on what was then known as the "old middle road," between Thirty-first and Thirty-fourth Streets, near the village of Kips Bay in New York City.

He worked alongside his employees, spending long hours at the job, and through his diligence and inventiveness, he improved methods of production and quality and bettered foreign imports. By 1856, he had turned his American glue business into a very profitable enterprise; sales soared and profits grew, and this is how he made his first million. So complete was his success that he won a monopoly in this trade chiefly because of the excellence of his products.

An innovative byproduct of the glue business was Peter's introduction in 1845 of a powdered gelatin dessert. He obtained the first patent (US Patent 4084) for the product, which became better known by the brand name Jell-O. Cooper described his dessert as a "transparent, concentrated substance containing all the ingredients fitting it for table use in a portable form, and requiring only the addition of hot water to dissolve it, so that it may be poured into moulds and when cold will be fit for use." From recipes hand-printed on little packets by Peter's wife Sarah, Victorian housewives could make lemon table jelly, blancmange, Charlotte Russe and snow pudding.

Peter counted among his professional affiliations membership in the prestigious General Society of Mechanics & Tradesmen of New York City (GSMT) and is listed in the membership archives on December 6, 1837, as a "Glue Maker," a tradesman term that Cooper preferred. GSMT is a mutual aid, educational and philanthropic organization that was founded in 1785 to promote the significance of manufacturing on the local economy.

It is interesting to note that Peter Cooper's only son, Edward, like his father made a number of important inventions, engineering improvements and special machinery used in the manufacture of glue. He was also prominent in politics and was mayor of New York City from 1879 to 1880.

THE IRONWORKS

Peter Cooper's success in business has been greatly attributed to his foresight to sell out at the right time and to move on to other ventures. Cooper was never discouraged and engaged in numerous iron ventures that proved successful.

In 1828, with two partners, he bought three thousand acres of land within the city limits of Baltimore, Maryland, and discovered iron ore on his property. Seeing the Baltimore & Ohio Railroad as a natural market for iron rails to be made from his ore, he erected the Canton Iron Works. His business expanded rapidly and included a wire factory in Trenton, New Jersey; three large blast furnaces in Philipsburg, Pennsylvania; a rolling mill factory at Thirty-third Street near Third Avenue in New York City; foundries in Durham, Pennsylvania; and iron mines in northern New Jersey.

He also bought the Andover mines in 1847 and built a railroad through a rough country for eight miles to bring the ore down from the furnaces at the rate of forty thousand tons per year. However, such severe demands were being made on the ore deposits that a new source of supply was sought.

Ringwood, New Jersey, one of the most celebrated iron ore properties in the East, was thrown on the market and bought at a sheriff's sale in 1854 by Peter Cooper and his son-in-law, Abram Stevens Hewitt, for $100,000. The twenty-two-acre property included the iron mines and a manor house, which after much improvement became the Cooper-Hewitts' second home. By this time, Cooper's glue factory and ironworks had made him one of New York's prominent millionaires, yet he still saw himself as a master craftsman, "a mechanic of New York."

Peter Cooper

The Tom Thumb: The First American Steam Locomotive

With a promise of the rapid completion of the Baltimore & Ohio Railroad, considerable excitement erupted among the landowners. However, there were greater problems with the railroad itself because the sharp turns in the road seemed to render it entirely useless for locomotive purposes. George Stephenson, an English engineer, declared it impossible for an engine to run on it. This was of great concern to Peter because the success of his land investment in the mining of iron ore for his Canton Iron Works greatly depended on the construction of the railroad. "I told the stockholders, who had become discouraged," Cooper said, "that if they would hold on a little while, I would put a small locomotive on the road, which I thought would demonstrate the practicality of using steam-engines on the road, even with all the sharp turns in it."

The locomotive Tom Thumb, because of its small size, was named after the well-known nineteenth-century British little person General Tom Thumb. It was designed to convince the owners of the Baltimore & Ohio Railroad to use steam engines. "When I completed the locomotive I invited the directors of the railroad to witness an experiment. Some thirty-six persons entered one of the passenger cars, and four rode on the locomotive and made the first passage, of thirteen miles, and turned all the short turns around the points of rocks in one hour and twelve minutes; and returned from Ellicott's Mills to Baltimore in fifty-seven minutes."

Peter Cooper's Tom Thumb proved that steam railroad was superior to horse-drawn transport:

> *This locomotive was built to demonstrate that cars could be drawn around short curves, beyond anything believed at that time to be possible. My contrivance saved this road from bankruptcy. This was the summer of 1830, but the triumph of the Tom Thumb engine was not altogether without a drawback. There were naysayers who wanted to see Cooper fail. The great stage proprietors of the day were Stockton and Stokes; and on the occasion a gallant gray, of great beauty and power, was driven by them from town, attached to another car on the second tract and met the engine at the Relay House, on its way back.*

William H. Brown, in *The History of the First Locomotives in America*, provided further account of the event:

Peter Cooper's Tom Thumb. *Courtesy of the Library of Congress.*

From this point, it was determined to have a race home; and, the start being even, away went horse and engine, the snort of one and the puff of the other keeping time and time. At first the gray had the best of it, for his steam would be applied to the greatest advantage on the instant, while the engine had to wait for the rotation of the wheels to set the blower to work.

The horse was perhaps a quarter of a mile ahead, when the safety-valve of the engine lifted, and the thin blue vapor issuing from it showed an excess of steam. The blower whistled, the steam blew off in vapory clouds, the pace increased, the passengers shouted, the engine gained on the horse, soon it lapped him—the silk was placed—the race was neck and neck, nose and nose—then the engine passed the horse, a great hurrah hailed the victory. But it was not repeated, for just at this time, when the gray master was about giving up, the band which drove the pulley, which moved the blower, slipped from the drum, the safety-valve ceased to scream, and the engine, for want of breath, began to wheeze and pant. Mr. Cooper, who was his own engineer and fireman, lacerated his hands in attempting to replace the band upon the wheel; in vain he tried to urge the fire with light wood: the horse gained on the machine and passed it, and although the band was presently replaced, and steam again did its best, the horse was too far ahead to be overtaken, and came in the winner of the race.

However, the real victory was with Mr. Cooper, notwithstanding. He had held fast to the faith that was in him, and had demonstrated its truth beyond peradventure. All honor to his name. Mr. Cooper's contrivance was one of the most potential instruments in making possible, in America, that vast system by which remote people were united by the railroads.

It is sufficient to say that the Tom Thumb would have won the race but for the leak in the boiler that caused excess pressure.

THE COOPERS MOVE TO GRAMERCY PARK AREA

Despite the pressing claims on business, Cooper did not neglect his family and was an attentive and loving family man. Then a prosperous industrialist, he set his goal to improve the family's living conditions.

Peter's first glue factory was conveniently located near his house on East Twenty-eighth Street and Fourth Avenue, next to the tracks of the New York & Harlem Railroad. The family endured considerable inconvenience from the sounds of the great herds of Texas Longhorn steers that were driven from the docks on the North River, up Irving Place to the stockyards and his glue factory in old Kips Bay village. Cooper's daughter, Amelia, remembered, "The cattle cars would often be left all night on the tracks in front of our house, and the bellowing of the animals disturbed my father."

A change of residence was obviously in order. Even though Peter Cooper had amassed quite a fortune, he continued his frugal ways and did not consider it suitable to build on the city's fashionable Fifth Avenue, where the wealthy had moved, as he considered the location too ostentatious for a workingman of humble origins and modest tastes. The quiet Gramercy Park area under development at the time seemed a more suitable environment for the new family home. Samuel Ruggles, the Donald Trump of his day, persuaded Cooper to purchase a big plot on the southwest corner of Lexington Avenue and Twenty-second Street in the Gramercy Park neighborhood. At first, Cooper thought of building on Fifth Avenue at Twenty-sixth Street. However, his mind was decidedly changed when Ruggles offered Cooper the land for the Lexington Avenue site for the same price he would have paid elsewhere. Cooper's decision was swayed by the fact that Ruggles had promised that a lot between Cooper's house and the park would be maintained as a rose garden, something Mrs. Cooper most assuredly approved of.

The area also attracted other notable New York citizens to the area, including Samuel Tilden, a noted Tammany politician and New York

Peter Cooper and his family. *Left to right*: Peter Cooper's daughter Sarah Amelia Cooper (later Sarah Amelia Hewitt), Peter Cooper, his son Edward Cooper and Sarah Bedell Cooper, Peter's wife. *Courtesy of The Cooper Union.*

governor from 1875 to 1877, whose mansion was built in the 1840s at 15 Gramercy Park South. Calvert Vaux "Victorianized" the façade, John LaFarge created stained-glass ceilings for the interior of the mansion and Italian carvers made the impressive fireplaces that eventually warmed the double parlors where plush fabrics adorned the exquisite furnishings. Today, this building is the headquarters of the National Arts Club, a private club whose membership includes artists and like-minded guests.

PETER COOPER'S STATELY HOME

In contrast to the opulent trappings and façades of neighboring mansions, Peter Cooper, always aware of his bourgeois status, did not count himself among the elite moguls of the day. Opting for a simpler structure, in 1850 he built a sturdy, four-story red brick building with about thirty-five rooms at 9 Lexington Avenue. For the first thirty years or so, the Cooper home had a high stoop front where, in Gramercy Park fashion, the family gathered and chatted with neighbors on warm evenings. Peter Cooper apparently liked to keep his family conveniently nearby, so when his son, Edward, married Cornelia Redmond in 1887, his father bought them property located at 11 Lexington Avenue.

Peter Cooper may have envisioned keeping his daughter, Amelia, close to him as well because his large but modest homestead had commodious accommodations for more than one family. When she married Abram Stevens Hewitt, the house was fitted up for the two families. Although they took their meals together, the Hewitts occupied the northern half and Peter Cooper the southern half of the house. In this congenial arrangement, the couple spent most of their winter season with the Coopers in Gramercy Park. Amelia probably took a great deal more kindly to this invitation (or parental order) than her husband, who eventually established their legal residence at the family's country estate, Ringwood Manor.

GRANDCHILDREN: ENCOURAGING INVENTION

The ambiance of the Cooper-Hewitt residence was enlivened by Amelia and Abram's brood of six lively and mischievous children—three boys (Peter Cooper; Edward Ringwood, nicknamed "Eddie"; and Erskine Hewitt), who were the bane of their mother's existence due to their youthful pranks and incorrigible behavior, and three rather dutiful daughters (Amy, Sarah Cooper and Eleanor Garnier).

Peter knew the value of tinkering and encouraged his children and grandchildren to use their imagination and to be inventive by using whatever they found at hand to create something. When they asked for toys, he would say, "I won't buy them, but I'll give you the tools to make them." To encourage the Hewitt boys to become inventors on their own, Cooper installed a workshop behind the house. Edward Ringwood remembered, "There was a yard in back of the house and a stable beyond that. Above the stable there was a workshop and a large gymnasium in which much time was spent with my brothers, Peter Cooper, who was older and Erskine who was younger."

Cooper was quite pleased with the family's new residence. A step up in the social arena of Gramercy Park, their new home provided a tranquil environment for his family and a rich intellectual life. Of course, it was pretty far uptown—"in the suburbs," some said.

AN EASY TOUCH

"Peter Cooper was a soft touch and his heart would melt with the slightest story of hardship," noted Edward Ringwood in his book *Those Were the Days.* "Women were more likely to succeed than men. One day my Sisters, Sally and Amy, dressed up as beggar-women, using the green shawls, that our Irish servants about their heads and shoulders when they went out. They rang the bell, told a heart-breaking tale of woe and got even more than they expected—two dollars—for which they were heartily ashamed and never knew whether their grandfather recognized them and their deception."

PROMINENT VISITORS

The commodious house on Lexington Avenue was the site of many lively dinners, receptions and entertainments. Cooper always gave a large party on his birthday, which was February 12, the same as Abraham Lincoln's. To be invited to it was considered the greatest possible feather in a young man's cap. Distinguished guests were among his many friends, and Gramercy Park neighbors regularly came to call on the revered industrialist. William Cullen Bryant, the renowned American poet, journalist and editor of the *New York Evening Post*, came to chat and recite poetry to his old friend. The parade of celebrated individuals also included Samuel Morse, the inventor and developer of the first successful telegraph in the United States. On any given evening, one might also find that the assembled dinner guests included Joseph Choate, lawyer and diplomat; Charles Dudley Warner, editor and essayist; and Whitelaw Reid, diplomat and journalist.

SEEKING PETER COOPER'S OPINION

Prominent inventors also sought Cooper's opinion. One day, Alexander Graham Bell came to visit, and he had with him a device called a telephone. Peter Cooper, who encouraged his grandchildren to be creative and inventive, invited his grandsons, Edward Ringwood and Peter Cooper, to go into his study to see it. After Bell showed them how it was made and how it worked, the Hewitt boys, enthusiastic juvenile inventors, rigged up their own telephone the day after they had seen one for the first time. Then they had to find a place to use it. They decided that they wanted to talk to their brother Erskine, who had scarlet fever and was quarantined. So, they ran the necessary wires under the hall carpet and got his nurse to run the wires into the room and up to his bed. The device worked perfectly, and when the doctor came to see Erskine, he was amazed and could scarcely believe that such a contrivance existed.

Thomas A. Edison brought his first phonograph to the house for Peter Cooper's inspection. Edison explained how his invention worked, and the Hewitt boys were soon at it again, rigging up a machine that squeakily repeated "hello" and a few other words.

The man who made the first typewriter, Christopher Latham Stokes, also brought it to Peter Cooper. According to Edward, "It was a poor affair, in a square wooden box. It wrote very badly and seemed to be so complicated and expensive to make that Peter Cooper did nothing about it. The typewriter was not developed to a practical point until years later."

It must have been a rare and privileged occasion when the great Norwegian artist Ole Bull entertained the Cooper-Hewitts. Like Cooper, Bull had the same modest, unassuming manner and took profound delight in playing his violin for the family. "His instrument was an Amati, fitted with a very flat bridge, which allowed him to play on all four strings at once. He walked up and down the house playing old-fashioned tunes, such as, 'Home Sweet Home,' and 'Coming Through the Rye' in full harmony as if the violin was a church organ."

When Red Cloud, chief of the Sioux Indians, came east to see President Grant about a treaty, he also came to a reception at the Cooper house dressed in full Indian costume. After he returned to Dakota, he sent Cooper an Indian buffalo robe. The leather was beautifully tanned and painted with the full history of the Sioux nation. Sadly, it was used in Peter Cooper's gig, where it was worn out and finally lost.

The Atlantic Cable

Peter Cooper had a hand in many of the country's scientific and industrial undertakings, and some of the first meetings of the New York, Newfoundland

& London Telegraph Company—which laid the Atlantic cable—took place at his home on Lexington Avenue. It may have been Cyrus West Field who was the originator of the project, but it was largely Mr. Cooper's money that kept it going during the years of experimentation.

Waxing nostalgic, Mr. Cooper, who was founding president of the company in 1854, recalled one of the very interesting episodes in his life and the personal efforts he made in behalf of the laying of the ocean cable. "An attempt had been made to put a line of telegraph cable across Newfoundland. Cyrus West Field, Moses Taylor, Marshal O. Roberts, Wilson G. Hunt, and myself completed that work across the island of Newfoundland, and then laid a cable across the Gulf of St. Lawrence, intending it as the beginning of a line from America to Europe by telegraphic communication." During this time, Samuel Morse, inventor of the telegraph machine, joined the investors. Despite broken cables, fierce storms and the initial difficulties in laying the cable, Cyrus Field and Peter Cooper both remained steadfast in this project. Cooper concluded, "After one form of difficulty after another had been surmounted, we found that more than ten years had passed before we got a cent in return, and we had been spending money the whole time. The work was finished at last, and I never have regretted it, although it was a terrible time to go through."

They were vindicated in 1866 when the successful connection of the first telegraphic cable was successfully laid across the Atlantic Ocean, shortening the time needed to communicate between the continents from several weeks to minutes. Much of the credit for the final success is due Cooper, who was president of the New York, Newfoundland & London Telegraph Company for twenty years and was its chief financier and supporter of Cyrus Field.

THE ATLANTIC CABLE PARADE

New Yorkers reacted with an enthusiastic outpouring of elation and with huge public celebrations in the same year, when Queen Victoria and President James Buchanan greeted each other across the great divide on the success of the new cable. To commemorate the great event, the Atlantic Cable Parade was held along Broadway, the most fashionable avenue of old New York. Along the route, spectators cheered on sailors from the *Niagara* who proudly carried aloft a model replica of their ship. The festivities continued in a celebration held at the Crystal Palace (the site of today's Bryant Park) in honor of the originator of the project, Cyrus Field. Considered an incredible feat at the time, the country's exultation took a downturn when the cable failed again and was unable to transmit further messages due to faulty insulation. The Civil War also intervened and silenced communication, and it took more years of struggle before all the problems could be resolved and a cable could finally go into continuous operation. This historical event, a "miracle," as some people referred to it, paved the way for the future of telegraphic communication between the United States and Europe.

THE PRINCE OF WALES' VISIT

Peter Cooper was the chief negotiator for many of old New York's stunning social events. In 1860, the Prince of Wales was sent by Queen Victoria on a state visit to Canada, but President Buchanan, a former minister to the Court of St. James, invited the prince to visit the United States. Peter Cooper intervened and called together a meeting of gentlemen at the Merchants Bank to invite the prince to New York City. After prolonged discussion, a number of gentlemen suggested a splendid ball, but the older, more influential leaders objected to this project on moral grounds, and it was decided to honor the prince with a banquet. However, the prince was eager for diversion other than the frequent banquets he had to endure during his travels. So, naturally, the invitation to yet another banquet was refused, but when the men in Cooper's group overcame their moral scruples, the invitation to a ball was accepted with alacrity.

Unprecedented enthusiasm greeted the Prince of Wales (later Edward VII), and three hundred people lined Broadway, from Bowling Green to the Fifth Avenue Hotel at Twenty-third Street. The prince met all the important men in the city, was escorted to all the important sights, was driven to see Cooper Union and Astor Library and was honored with a torchlight parade by the fire department.

The grandest ball held in New York took place on October 12, 1860, at the Academy of Music, where a dance floor had been installed over the stage and orchestra. The academy was packed to suffocation with four thousand elegant New Yorkers eager to see the prince. The problem of selecting dancing partners for the prince stirred up a tempest, but to his credit, the prince patiently danced with innumerable socially eligible ladies. The chairman of the ball, Peter Cooper, and his wife were counted among the celebrated guests. Eleanor Garnier Hewitt remembered, "It was with great difficulty that Peter Cooper was persuaded to wear a dress suit for the occasion. He considered a dress coat the livery of fashion. However, the argument which made him yield was that he would not be honoring the Queen of England, and she would be annoyed. Peter Cooper said that he would never do anything to displeasure a lady, and he ordered a suit, but that was the one and only time he wore it."

It was a night to remember. Never had New York seen such a brilliant and beautiful assemblage of men and women, who would always count the ball as one of the great events of their lives.

THE PETER COOPER PILLOW

Peter Cooper's inventive faculty was never at rest, and out of personal necessity, he came up with an ingenious device to accommodate his bony and rigid physique, an air-filled pillow with a center hole in it that he used to relieve the pressure on his bones as he drove around town in his old black buggy. Edward Ringwood remembered, "He took the pillow to formal dinners and parties to provide relief from wood chairs, which were uncomfortably hard. Cooper convinced his friend, Charles Goodyear, to produce the air pillow, which was dubbed, 'The Peter Cooper,' for public sale."

COOPER'S INTEREST IN EDUCATION

Cooper became a wealthy man, but prosperity did not dry up his benevolence. Despite Cooper's commitment to his various business enterprises, he did find time to engage in civic duties and was an early advocate of paid police and fire departments, sanitary water conditions and public schools. Education was paramount on his agenda, and he became an active member of the Public School Society and, subsequently, of the board of education.

His interest in education began while serving as the assistant alderman of the New York Common Council, and he led the campaign of the Free

Schools Society, organized to give free instruction to New York's children. One can imagine how the lively conversation at the Coopers' dinner table often gave way to the subject closest to Peter Cooper's heart: his dream to establish a "free" arts and science institution for young men and women of modest means. Peter Cooper never forgot what it was like to be denied a formal education, and being interested in the welfare of the working class, his heart was set on making sure that no other man or woman would experience such a loss. On Sundays, Peter went to pastor Henry Whitney Bellow's All Souls Unitarian Church on the corner of Twentieth Street and Fourth Avenue (now Park Avenue South), where the charismatic minister was a founder of the philosophical movement pragmatism. The relationship between Cooper and Bellows was a close one, so much so that he frequently talked with his minister about his dream of building a free college.

Abram Stevens Hewitt, Cooper's son-in-law and trusted business confidant, brought the plan for a free technical college before Peter Cooper. The fortune Cooper had amassed from his glue business and ironworks, his patent inventions and his real estate investments provided Cooper with a financial means to invest his money in The Cooper Union, commonly called at that time "Cooper Institute." He modeled the Union after the École Polytechnique (Polytechnical School) in Paris. It was to be the crowning glory of his life.

THE COOPER UNION CORNERSTONE LAID

After years of planning and obstacles, Peter Cooper's great vision was fulfilled when the cornerstone was laid in 1854, and in 1859, The Cooper Union for the Advancement of Science and Art was charted by the state legislature and named Cooper Union. It was one of the first institutions in the country to offer a free education to students who, like Cooper, were the sons and daughters of the working class.

Cooper erected an imposing six-story Italianate building, designed by Frederick A. Peterson, between Third and Fourth Avenues at Astor Place in New York City. This is the very same site where Cooper had at one time operated a grocery business in the early days of his entrepreneurial struggles. Perhaps that is why he at first considered providing space on the street level for retail stores. In the old days, there were only four floors devoted

Cooper Union for the Advancement of Science & Art, located at Third and Fourth Avenues, Astor Place, Seventh Street, New York City. *Courtesy of the Library of Congress, Historic American Buildings Survey.*

to classes, and it was necessary to rent out the street level and also the first story, where at one time one of the tenants was a dentist who specialized in tooth extraction with laughing gas. Cooper did not escape criticism. Some deemed his vision preposterous and impractical, and a few thought him a "snake in the grass" for using shops on the ground floor of Cooper Union as a way to skirt taxes. Cooper evidently charmed his critics, and some of them eventually became donors.

That manner of raising income through rentals ended when sufficient income enabled the Union to use all the building's space for educational purposes. Further endorsing the "no rental policy," Cooper's son-in-law, Abram Stevens Hewitt, supported the college's mission to be a truly tuition-free institution.

THE COOPER UNION OPENING

Commemorating the building's upcoming opening, the *New York Daily Times'* January 21, 1853 headline read, "The People's Union," and noted, "To Science and Art is dedicated the noble structure in the course of erection on Astor Place by Mr. Peter Cooper; and in such a living monument, the name of the benevolent founder will be worthily perpetuated with the undying arts. While seeking 'the moral, mental and physical improvement of his race,' he has secured a posthumous fame more noble and enduring than the powerful, but self-idolizing founders of useless pyramids."

The Cooper Union was the nation's first free institute and the first to provide adult education in the United States for gifted students in the fields of engineering, architecture and domestic science.

To support the floors and make the building fireproof, some of Cooper's own wrought-iron beams were produced at the Cooper Hewitt & Company ironworks at Trenton, New Jersey, with special machinery from England that could roll beams the size required. However, building costs being what they were at the time and pressed financially, the building of the Union was forestalled.

As soon as the first story of The Cooper Union was laid, John Jacob Astor, who was then building the Astor Library nearby, saw these beams and asked Peter Cooper to roll beams for the Astor Library. Cooper's grandson, Edward Ringwood, recalled, "My grandfather said that the beams for Cooper Union must be finished first. However, Mr. Astor would not wait; he offered a price which Peter Cooper felt he could not refuse. So he rolled the beams for the Astor Library, which was the first building in America completed with iron beams. When accounts were made up, Mr. Cooper found that he had cleared the entire cost of the machinery from this one order—six thousand dollars."

When The Cooper Union was erected, passenger elevators did not exist in New York City, but provision had been made in the great visionary's original design for a special elevator shaft. At that time, the architect, Frederick A. Petersen, insisted that there was no elevator that would do the job. Obviously, Peter Cooper's mechanical mind saw that higher buildings would demand mechanical lifts. He saw his prophecy come true, and an elevator was later installed in the place he had provided. Cooper's son, Edward, eventually designed a vertical steam engine with hoisting drum, which was used satisfactorily as power for the elevator for more than forty years. Later, it was taken out and replaced with electric drive.

Cooper Union may not have been so imposing an institution as the "Collegiate Gothic" (Columbia College), but it was a school in which New

York City took pride. Reflecting on his unfulfilled desire for a formal education, Peter Cooper addressed The Cooper Union graduating class of 1871:

> *There being no free schools by day, nor any night schools whatsoever, I found it far more difficult to learn what I wanted to know, than to be industrious, temperate and prudent. Hence, I decided, if I should prosper in the acquisition of worldly goods, to found an institution to which all young people of the working-classes, who desired to be good citizens and rise in life, could resort without money and without price, in order to acquire that knowledge of their business and science which, in these days, is absolutely indispensable to a successful career.*

The Cooper Union's open-door policy offered free education for young men and women who qualified independent of their race, religion, sex, wealth or social status. It was an institution of practical knowledge in the arts, technologies and sciences, with due attention to fostering social responsibility.

From the beginning, Cooper Union was particularly ahead of its time in opening its doors to female students. In Cooper's day, women had few opportunities for gainful employment, and he was particularly concerned about their plight. Cooper said that opening enrollment to women created a "new pathway to useful studies for women who unable and unwilling to become mere drudges in servile occupations, and for the meanest pittance, would be doomed otherwise to sell themselves at the matrimonial altar, or resign themselves to a life of cheerless activity and poverty." Cooper's concerns were fulfilled when students in the Women's Art School were able take courses and master their craft and, in other departments, perfect their clerical skills.

During the last year of Peter Cooper's life, he visited all the rooms and classes with his grandson, Edward Ringwood:

> *When he came to the new typewriting class, he stood in the doorway and surveyed the thirty girls working at their machines. Then he turned to me and said, "This is the last class I shall see established and it is the first of its kind in the country. These girls are learning a new trade, which will be followed by many people. It will earn the living of numerous individuals. This is the newest profession and I am glad to have seen it started here. When telegraphy was beginning I had a class here. When wood engraving became an important art I furnished a class for it. And again, when photography became a commercial art, we began instruction in it here. I will go my way now, feeling that, at the Cooper Union, we have kept pace with the times."*

Left: The clock that adorns
The Cooper Union for the
Advancement of Science & Art.
*Courtesy of the Library of Congress,
Historic American Buildings Survey.*

Below: An artist's sketch of the
engraving room at The Cooper
Union. *Courtesy of the Library of
Congress, Historic American Buildings
Survey.*

An interior view of
The Cooper Union for
the Advancement of
Science & Art. *Courtesy
of the Library of Congress,
Historic American
Buildings Survey.*

THE UNION'S GREAT HALL

The reading room, library and picture gallery were among the first to be available to the general public, and the large auditorium, the Great Hall, was associated with some of the most epic events in the metropolis. In 1860, Abraham Lincoln framed his "Right Makes Right" speech as an opportunity to continue his famous "debates" with his archrival, Democrat Stephen A. Douglas, on the question of slavery. That memorable speech, now referred to as the "Cooper Union Address," served to launch Abraham Lincoln's presidential campaign, and it also helped to transform the candidate from an unknown western lawyer into the leading Republican contender.

Peter Cooper had insisted that the large 3,500-seat auditorium be located in the expansive basement facility as a safety measure. He believed that in the event of fire, panicked crowds were less likely to trample one another because when all the entrances to the spacious lecture hall were thrown open, it could be emptied in minutes. To further comfort the students and general public,

The philosophical lecture room at The Cooper Union for the Advancement of Science & Art. *Courtesy of the Library of Congress, Historic American Buildings Survey.*

Cooper also installed a gigantic fan that circulated air through small vents in the seats; the ventilating system continued to work for the next hundred years.

Cooper Union's long reputation as a political arena set the stage for future presidents who also spoke at the Great Hall, including Ulysses S. Grant, William Howard Taft and Theodore Roosevelt, to name a few. Other presidents continued to choose the Great Hall as a platform for political discussion. Bill Clinton spoke on May 12, 1993, about reducing the federal deficit and again on May 23, 2006, and he was the keynote speaker at The Cooper Union's 147th Commencement.

According to Allan Nevins in the book *Abram S. Hewitt with Some Account of Peter Cooper*, "Cooper Union blazed a new path in the education of hardworking mechanics and struggling youth with practical training in science and mechanics with an inspiring instruction in art. In its early history it was the embodiment of Peter Cooper's benevolent impulse and Abram Stevens Hewitt's brain."

THE COOPER UNION ALUMNI

Since 1859, Cooper Union has educated thousands of artists, architects and engineers, many of them leaders in their fields. Over the years, students who trained there include the Irish-born American sculptor Augustus Saint-Gaudens (1848–1907), whose statue of Peter Cooper stands in front of The Cooper Union library today. He also designed historic monuments commemorating heroes of the American Civil war, including the grand equestrian monument of William Tecumseh Sherman astride his horse (*Winged Victory*) on Grand Army Plaza, between Fifty-ninth and Sixtieth Streets on Fifth Avenue in New York City.

The list of notable alumni is far too extensive to record here but includes Milton Glaser, graphic designer, founder of *New York* magazine and creator of the I Love New York logo; Victor Papanek, early proponent of ecologically and socially responsible design; and George Segal, pop art sculptor.

I remember the Vera brand. A fine arts graduate of Cooper Union, Vera Neumann (1907–1993) is, to fashionable women, one of the most recognized scarf and product designers, a woman who became known professionally as just "Vera." She tagged her charming floral and geometric designs with her signature logo of a ladybug, which to Neumann symbolized happiness.

A corridor through the classrooms, Cooper Union for the Advancement of Science & Art.
Courtesy of the Library of Congress, Historic American Buildings Survey.

ESTABLISHING A TRUST

The seeds of philanthropy planted so early by Peter Cooper inspired the Cooper-Hewitt family throughout their lifetime to establish a sounder foundation for Cooper Union's survival. In 1898, Eleanor Garnier Hewitt and Sarah Cooper Hewitt joined with their father, mother, brothers, sister and cousin in executing a trust deed by which a trust fund, provided by Mr. Cooper during his lifetime for their support, should be transferred to Cooper Union as they passed away. By this gift, Peter Cooper and his descendants created an endowment fund to which Andrew Carnegie contributed in an amount up to $600,000, equal to what the Cooper and Hewitt families would furnish. The Cooper-Hewitt family fund was at that time invested in the block on Lexington Avenue, running from Forty-second Street to Forty-third Street, one of the prime real estate locations near Grand Central Station in the heart of New York City. The Cooper Union made a deal whereby the Chrysler Building was built on this plot, and the Union receives a large ground rent for this property.

On the occasion of another visit to Cooper Union, Edward Ringwood remarked, "It was my father's greatest joy—as well as my own—that we have been able to see the vision of Peter Cooper carried forward." The Cooper Union building was declared a National Historic Landmark in 1961 and a New York City Landmark in 1965.

Peter Cooper was unstoppable. In the broader field of national politics, he supported the Greenback Party and consented to run on its ticket in the 1876 presidential election, but he received less than 1 percent of the vote. At the age of eighty-five, Cooper was the oldest person ever nominated by a political party for president of the United States. The election was won by Rutherford Hayes of the Republican Party.

THE COOPER UNION MUSEUM

In Cooper's day, the only museum of any account in New York City was the New York Historical Society. Although P.T. Barnum called his emporium "Barnum's American Museum," it offered the credulous public a large menagerie of exotica, oddities and gadgets. It was always Peter Cooper's vision to have a museum in Cooper Union, but it took nearly fourteen years after Cooper's time for the museum to become a reality. The creation of the museum is fully explored in the third part of this book, "The Hewitt Sisters."

SARAH BEDELL COOPER

Peter Cooper shared a long and happy married life with Sarah Bedell. He never spoke of his wife without emotion, which he expressed in a poignant display of reverie. And so it was that when Sarah Bedell died on the fifty-sixth anniversary of her wedding day, December 1869, Cooper attributed all his highest happiness and most of his success in life to the sterling qualities of character in his wife. The brokenhearted giant succumbed with sadness and said to a friend at her funeral, "Yes, she has gone who was 'the day star,' the solace and inspiration of my life. During a business career of nearly sixty years, I was cheered, comforted, sustained, and encouraged by the greatest of human blessings—a diligent, wise, industrious, faithful, and affectionate wife, and a woman of superior moral qualities, and precisely that fitness and training that made her a worthy and most efficient help-mate."

THE FIRST CITIZEN OF OLD NEW YORK

Without the comfort and companionship of his faithfully devoted wife, Peter Cooper rallied on with devoted interest in his family and enterprises. He seemed to be in excellent health for one of his great age, and so, to celebrate his birthday on January 12, 1882, Mr. and Mrs. Abram Hewitt gave a dinner party at their Lexington Avenue mansion. However, the accolades and celebration honoring Cooper, the "first citizen of Old New York," turned to mourning on April 4, 1883, when the venerable philanthropist died peacefully at home at the age of ninety-two. "I still feel somewhat in debt to the world," was one of his last sayings.

Many friends called at the Cooper residence to express their sympathy to the bereaved family. The long list of visitors from both political and artistic circles included Albert Bierstadt, the famous Hudson River School painter; David Dudley Field, United States jurist; John Jay, first chief justice of the United States; Henry Bergh, the social reformer and founder of the American Society for the Prevention of Cruelty to Animals (ASPCA); Joseph H. Choate, the United States diplomat; and Hamilton Fish, United States secretary of state.

It was said that he was the oldest inhabitant of old New York, which had grown during his lifetime from 40,000 inhabitants to 2 million. Some 12,000 citizens turned out to honor the great industrialist and drew thousands of draymen and shop girls, who mingled with millionaires and passed by his coffin. In respectful reverence, part of the façade of Peter Cooper's Cooper Union was festooned in black drape, and public offices of New York City were closed. Great delegations of many societies paid their respects.

A feature story in the *New York Times* on April 7, 1883, reported, "Members of the glue trade regarded the death of Peter Cooper as bereaving us of one, who, by his inventions, ingenuity and wholesome business principles, was an example and ornament to our trade, and one who possessed of all those noble qualities that call forth our highest admiration and respect."

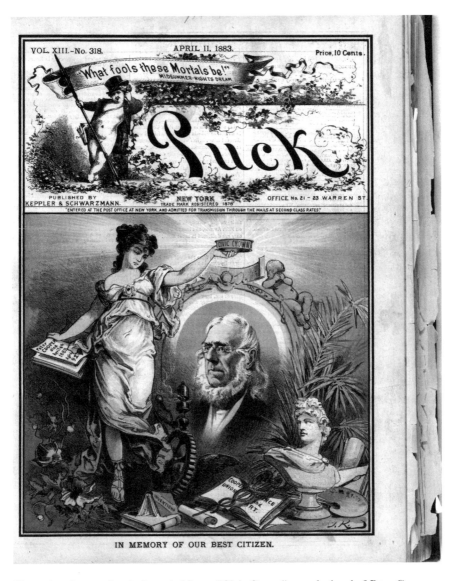

Illustration shows a female figure holding a "Civic Crown" over the head of Peter Cooper; she is also holding a ledger that states, "Peter Cooper died April 4th 1883 Age 92." Among the books and papers at the bottom is one that states, "Cooper Union—Science and Art." *Courtesy of the Library of Congress.*

A delegation of Cooper Union alumni served as honor guard, and flags were lowered to half-mast as Cooper's coffin was escorted to Greenwood Cemetery in Brooklyn.

In 1874, Cooper had said, "I have always recognized that the object of business is to make money in an honorable manner. I have endeavored to remember that the object of life is to do good." To this creed he remained faithful.

PART II

Abram Stevens Hewitt

America's Foremost Private Citizen

To understand Abram Steven Hewitt's character, one only needs to see that he came of the best stock on both sides, combining as he did with both English and French qualities.

It was typical at the time that French names went through many changes. Abram Stevens Hewitt's lineage is directly linked to the names Garnier and Gurnee, which in historical data appear to be used interchangeably. On his application for membership in the Huguenot Society of America, Abram Stevens Hewitt in his own handwriting listed Isaac Garnier as his great-great-grandfather, François Garnier as his great-grandfather and Francis Gurnee as his grandfather.

Hewitt's ancestry traces back to the Revocation of the Edict of Nantes by Louis IV in 1685. Because of this act of folly and tyranny, multitudes of aristocrats and the ablest artisans and most capable citizens of France left their native land, never to return. Among those was Isaac Garnier of French Huguenot stock, originally from La Rochelle, Île de Ré, France, who settled in New Rochelle, New York. Soon after the death of Isaac Garnier, his elder son, François Garnier, moved to Haverstraw, New York, and was counted among the largest landowners in the region. In this time or soon after, the family surname name was modified by the usage of the English-speaking community and Anglicized to the form of "Gurnee," and it was recorded as such in the French Church in New York.

François Garnier was the first to use the new "Gurnee" spelling, and his son, named Francis Gurnee, was Hewitt's grandfather. Francis later married

Eleanor Garnier
Hewitt. *Courtesy of
The Cooper Union.*

a young woman, recorded in the Huguenot records as Eleanor Parcelle (1746–unknown). The Gurnee union produced a son, William F. Gurnee, and a daughter, Ann Gurnee, the mother of Abram Stevens Hewitt, the future mayor of New York City. The Garnier name appears as Eleanor Garnier Hewitt's middle name, yet in one portrait she is identified as Eleanor Gurnee Hewitt. Clearly, the surname Garnier and Gurnee were used interchangeably over time.

Hewitt came from a long line of cabinetmaker craftsmen. Abram's father, John Hewitt, had been trained by his grandfather in the fine art of cabinet craftsmanship. While still in his teens, John already held his first-class certificate as a cabinetmaker, but the talented young man also trained as a mechanic and pattern maker. He emigrated from Penkridge, Staffordshire, England, to the United States in 1796, and along with other skilled English mechanics, John worked on several projects, the most significant of which was the first steam engine built in the United States. With the work completed, the young English mechanic decided to stay in the young republic and returned to cabinetmaking.

The thriving environs of old New York were the ideal setting for commerce, and in 1805, John Hewitt, scarcely twenty-eight years old, opened a small shop at 191 Water Street between Beekman and Burling Slips. He set himself on a daring course as a purveyor of fine, handcrafted furniture. Some say that Hewitt's reputation as a craftsman and the excellent quality of his period furniture pieces rivaled the work of Duncan Phyfe.

During the halcyon days of Hewitt's flourishing cabinetmaking business, he exported extensively to the South, and the principal outlets of that market were Savannah and St. Marys, Georgia. Hewitt's furniture business was operating on a steady course of production, but his business decline in 1802 was brought about by an unexpected epidemic of yellow fever in the South, and the sales he garnered resulted in meager compensation. Even Hewitt's famous competitor Duncan Phyfe sold furniture at great loss, far below its worth.

JOHN HEWITT AND ANN GURNEE

After only a few years of marriage, John Hewitt's first wife, Phoebe Tiemann, whom he had married in 1802, died along with their two infant sons, John and James, perhaps during the yellow fever epidemic in the South. On October 31, 1808, the widower married Ann Gurnee, daughter of a farmer, in Haverstraw, New York, a young woman of French Huguenot ancestry. She was a descendant of the Garniers.

ABRAM STEVENS HEWITT FAMILY TREE

GRANDPARENTS

John Hewitt (1751–1803)

BORN: Knutsford, Cheshire
United Kingdom

Cabinetmaker

English ancestry

Married Sarah Tomlinson
(1742–1806)

Son of John and Sarah

• John Hewitt

Francis Gurnee (1735–1822)

BORN: Haverstraw, New York,
United States

Landowner

French Huguenot ancestry:

Great-great-grandfather, Isaac Garnier

Great-grandfather, François Garnier

Married Eleanor Parcelle
(1746–unknown)

Daughter of Francis and Eleanor

• Ann Gurnee

PARENTS

John Hewitt (1777–1857)

BORN: Staffordshire,
United Kingdom

Mechanic and cabinetmaker

Immigrated to the
United States in 1796

Ann Gurnee (1784–1870)

BORN: Haverstraw, New York

French Huguenot ancestry

John Hewitt and Ann Gurnee married in 1808 and had seven children, including son Abram Stevens Hewitt.

Abram Stevens Hewitt

Abram Stevens Hewitt (1822–1903)

BORN: Haverstraw, New York

Mayor of New York from 1887 to 1888

Sarah Amelia Cooper (1830–1912)

BORN: New York City

Daughter of Peter Cooper

Abram Stevens Hewitt and Sarah Amelia Cooper married in 1855 and had six children.

Amelia Bowman "Amy" Hewitt (1856–1922)

Sarah Cooper Hewitt (1858–1930)

Peter Cooper Hewitt (1861–1921)

Eleanor Garnier/Gurnee Hewitt (1864–1924)

Edward Ringwood Hewitt (1866–1957)

Erskine Hewitt (1871–1938)

Peter Cooper Hewitt (1861–1921) and Lucy Bond Work (1861–1934) married in 1887 and had no children. Peter and Lucy divorced in 1918, and Peter married Maryon Denning Bruguiere (née Jeanne Andrews, 1884–1939) and had a daughter, Ann Cooper Hewitt (1914–1956)

Edward Ringwood Hewitt (1866–1957) and Mary Emma Ashley (1866–1946) married 1892 and had four children—sons Abram Stevens II and Ashley Cooper and daughters Lucy and Candace.

Amelia Bowman "Amy" Hewitt (1856–1922) and Dr. James Olive Green (1842–1924) married in 1886 and had two children: son Norvin Hewitt (1893–1955), who married Irene Pierce (daughter of Irene Tewksbury and Arthur Clay Pierce) in 1922, and daughter Eleanor Margaret Green (1895–1966), who married Christian Adolph Georg, HRH Prince Viggo of Denmark (1893–1970) in 1924. She acquired the title Eleanor Margaret, HRH Princess Viggo of Denmark.

AMERICA'S FOREMOST PRIVATE CITIZEN

Abram Stevens Hewitt's life is a quintessentially American story—the triumph of a rags-to-riches maverick who became one of the most celebrated men of industry, politics and philanthropy. Like Peter Cooper, Abram Stevens Hewitt was a self-made man who grew up poor and in humble circumstances. The kindred spirit that developed between Abram Hewitt and Peter Cooper lasted throughout their lifetimes through invention and enterprises. Hewitt's connection to the Cooper circle was also strengthened by his business partnership with Cooper's son, Edward, in Cooper Hewitt & Company. His marriage to Cooper's daughter, Amelia, reinforced his fate as the second important patriarch in the Cooper-Hewitt dynasty in New York.

The many great works of Abram Stevens Hewitt were remarkable achievements during his lifetime. However, he considered the most successful feature of his career to be the organization of The Cooper Union, which he aided Peter Cooper in founding in 1859. Like Peter Cooper, Hewitt realized the hardships a boy without means would experience in trying to get a technical education. The Cooper Union may have been Peter Cooper's great vision, but it was Abram Hewitt who took a leading part in establishing the "free" college, supervised its construction and directed all of its education and finances, serving as its president for more than forty years.

Abram Hewitt's reputation as the foremost ironmaster in America secures for him an important place in the successful industrial revolution in the United States. He was president of the American Institute of Mining Engineers in 1876 and again in 1890. In the latter year, he was awarded the Bessemer Gold Medal by the Iron & Steel Institute. From the business offices of Cooper Hewitt & Company, at 17 Burling Slip, New York City, Hewitt directed his large business interests. He was a director of many concerns, including the United States Steel Corporation, the New Jersey and New York Railroad Company, the American Bridge Company, the Alabama Consolidated Coal and Iron Company and several banks.

Hewitt's reputation in business and political circles in New York equaled his nominations. In 1874, he was elected to the United States Congress and continued in that capacity until he defeated Theodore Roosevelt in the campaign for mayor of New York. Due to his deep-rooted sense of honor and honesty, and the fact that he could not be influenced, he served but one year as mayor of New York (1887–88). Hewitt incurred the animosity of

Abram Stevens Hewitt.
*Courtesy of the Library of
Congress.*

the Democratic Party, the autocratic institution of Tammany Hall, and that
contributed to his one term in office.

Henry B. Adams in his autobiography, *The Education of Henry Adams*,
pronounced Hewitt "the most useful man in Washington," and he claimed
to know of "no other man who had done so much."

ABRAM HEWITT'S EARLY YEARS

Though hardship dogged Abram Stevens Hewitt's early life, his strong moral
fiber and determination to succeed were two of his greatest assets.

Early on, when Abram's father, John Hewitt, and his family lived on Water Street, his home was also a cabinetmaker's workshop. One night, the house burned to the ground, and as many of his debtors had failed to pay him their obligations, this double loss left him penniless. The family was rescued from poverty by an uncle, who carted them all back to Haverstraw, providing the family with a roof over their heads. They lived in this rural hamlet in a home that was nothing more than a log cabin. Under these rather meager circumstances, Abram Stevens Hewitt was born on July 31, 1822, on a stony farm in the Mount Ivy section of the town. There he grew up, spending his summers working on the farm and his winters attending the public schools in New York.

In later life, when Abram had achieved success and wealth, he recalled with a certain degree of sadness, "My family seldom ate meat except at Christmas and holidays and much to my chagrin I wore makeshift garments." His mother had been given a bolt of coarse yellow-green wool baize cloth to make his clothing, and you can imagine the jeers and bullying he endured from his school chums, who used to call him "Baizy." He loathed the color for his entire life.

After many years in Haverstraw, the year 1824 saw some recovery. Things seemed to change for the better when John Hewitt received an award for his patented device for a sleigh-type bed at the New York Fair of 1829. By 1830, the family had moved back to New York City, and Hewitt had reentered business as a "patent bedstead manufacturer" at 20 Hudson Street.

Despite his narrow circumstances, Abram had the innate advantage of his steadfast character and a brilliant mind. At thirteen, he began his education in the public schools of New York City, attending Public School 10 at Duane Street and receiving an education in the classics and mathematics. As a result of his intelligence and book learning, he excelled in his studies.

He was a diligent scholar and spent his free time in downtown Crosby Street, where the General Society of Mechanics & Tradesmen building was originally located. In the 1885 Centennial Celebration, Abram recalled a visit to the society with his father, John Hewitt, who had been initiated as a member in 1810. "When I was a boy eleven years of age, my father took me by the hand and led me up into the Apprentice Library. For the first time in my life, I saw books beyond the wildest dreams of my fancy." There Abram indulged his passion for reading in one of the richest collections of books in New York. Abram began with *The Tempest* and proceeded to read all the plays of Shakespeare. Reading proved an advantage to employment, and he was able to earn money tutoring children of well-to-do friends.

Although his family could not afford college, in 1839 Abram won in a competition two scholarships for four years' tuition at Kings College (now Columbia University), which was originally located downtown in the financial enclaves of old New York City. Throughout Abram's college career, he stood at the head of his class and was considered to be a brilliant student. Using the astute memory he had developed by his extensive reading, he took near verbatim notes in lectures, and during those college days, he paid his own expenses by tutoring and dealing in books. Still further, he increased his income by competing for and winning every prize offered in mathematics, as well as winning three prizes for Greek competitions. When he was twenty years old, he graduated in 1842 from his alma mater Kings College with high rank, magna cum laude. At commencement, he was Greek salutatorian, the highest honor for a graduating student.

In order to support himself, he chose teaching as his profession, and by 1843, he was acting professor of mathematics. Pressing on with his education, Hewitt studied an additional year for his law degree, and in spite of admission to the New York Bar, he never practiced law as an attorney. However, one can surmise that his law education served him well later in life, for he proved to be an astute businessman of unusual ability and boundless energy.

To achieve his high scholastic standing, Hewitt pushed himself beyond the brink of normalcy, and the additional burden of work responsibilities took its toll on his health. With the combined strain of his teaching position and at the same time tutoring in mathematics, plus the intense study of law, Abram's eyesight began to fail, and he was ordered by a doctor to stop all these activities.

THE COOPER-HEWITT LIAISON

The saga of the Cooper-Hewitt dynasty took a leap into the future through serendipitous circumstances. In one of Abram's efforts to support himself, he was engaged as a tutor to Peter Cooper's son, Edward, who had fallen behind in his studies due to illness. The instruction was given in Cooper's stately home at 9 Lexington Avenue. By this seemingly casual mentoring arrangement began the Cooper-Hewitt relationship that would forever tie one family with the other over a period of one hundred years.

It is possible to speculate that when Abram was occupied with tutoring Edward at the Cooper mansion, there may have been an occasion to see or be introduced to Peter Cooper's daughter, Amelia. However, at that time, it was of no consequence because Amelia, the future Mrs. Abram Stevens Hewitt, was a rosy, twelve-year-old girl in pigtails. Abram and Edward, who were in their early twenties, young men on the brink of their careers, most likely took no particular notice of her. That attitude on the part of Abram was to change dramatically, and romance blossomed several years later when he saw the lovely young lady at seventeen in the full bloom of her feminine charms.

TRAVELS TO EUROPE

After graduation from college, Abram, like Edward, was anxious to travel. Due to the fact that he was unable to study because of his poor eyesight, the timing was ideally suited for convalescing. However, unlike Cooper, Hewitt had to rely on his own financial resources. Abram had managed to save nearly $1,000, a remarkable sum for the time, but he was interested in securing a more stable financial situation. So, he obtained a letter of introduction from Samuel J. Tilden to Senator Silas Write in Washington, D.C., and tried in vain to get dispatches from the State Department to take abroad. Despite this disappointment, Abram was solvent enough to make plans with Edward to visit Europe.

With high spirits, the two young men made arrangements to take the Grand Tour, a custom at the time, and went abroad from 1843 to 1844. With the portent of an adventure, they embarked for Europe on a journey that was described by the young students as "an eventful trip that augmented the classical education they had received at Kings College." They visited major cities, particularly in France, Germany and Italy, and along the way they collected souvenirs and books.

In later years, Abram's daughter, Eleanor Garnier, commented on this trip and referred to her French-speaking father: "My father's facility for languages made his journey particularly enriching and increased his appreciation of art." Abram's rich Huguenot heritage was a definite advantage, as was the fact that he was proficient in French, Latin and Greek.

At the completion of their tour, the young men returned from Europe on October 10, 1844, from Leghorn (Livorno), Italy. Edward and Abram took passage on the *Alabamian*, an old sailing ship that was laden with a valuable cargo of marble and silks. The two young travelers had no idea about the perils of the voyage that lay before them and took off with the high hopes of youthful adventure.

Near Fatal Shipwreck

Upon returning to New York in 1844, before passing the Straits of Gibraltar, the ship encountered a severe gale. This followed with a double blow on November 14 off the Western Islands, yet Abram recalled, "The ship rode out the gale admirably."

This reprieve was short-lived, as the fearful seas further buffeted the ship and threatened its seaworthiness. However, a fair wind eventually prevailed, and safe passage was experienced until the ship was off the coast of Cape May, New Jersey. Unexpectedly, heavy gales broke on every side of the ship with dreadful fury, and the cargo shifted with the rolling so that the ship leaked very badly. The *Alabamian* managed to approach Delaware Breakwater with the aid of a pilot boat, but the gale was more dreadful than the first, and the ship was driven out to sea. The battered ship quickly took on water, and the crew and passengers bailed at the pumps day and night. A brig was then sighted about three or four miles to the windward. Though the *Alabamian* made signals of distress, no attention was paid to them. It seemed like all was lost.

As he realized that the hapless ship's chance of deliverance was running out, Captain Hitchcock exclaimed, "God grant that he may never need that aid which he now refuses to afford!" So mighty was the power of the sea and the bombardment to the boat that Captain Hitchcock surmised that the situation was futile and decided to abandon ship. He told Abram to advise Edward.

Abram dutifully followed orders. "I went below to inform Edward that the Captain has ordered us to leave the ship in a half hour."

Lying about in his bunk in a nonchalant manner, Edward asked, "Are you sure that he said a half hour?"

"Yes," replied Abram.

"Then wake me up in fifteen minutes."

Edward never hurried or had any nerves, but with the urgency of the situation, the captain was already drawing lots for the boats. One was in good condition, and the other was a longboat that had been used as a pigpen and was more or less in rotten condition. First Mate Benson drew the good boat and the captain the pigpen. As fate would have it, a few passengers, including the two young men and the captain, went adrift in the little pigsty boat, which had no sails and drifted with the current away from the sinking ship. In this perilous adventure, the pigpen was too rotten to be rowed and was at the mercy of the ocean.

The sea was so high that more than half of the time the pigsty boat was hidden from view; being sighted by a rescue ship was less than likely. After the captain's solemn invocation "to Him who rules the storm, either to grant them salvation or to smooth their path and return home," he faithfully kept watch. The unprecedented swells of the sea and battering by high winds had forced the abandonment of this ship and cast the two young men adrift in a rotten boat with scant hope of rescue.

During the whole of this ominous and seemingly hopeless scene, Edward and Abram thought of home, friends and family, and tears welled up in their eyes as they pondered the seemingly bleak fate that lay ahead.

Miraculously, early in the afternoon, First Mate Benson in icy and violent winds managed to row his boat north to get in the track of ships, as the boat was then south of the regular shipping lanes. This course of action enabled Benson to reach the *Atalanta*, manned by Captain George B. Raymond of New York. Captain Raymond at once got his ship underway and sailed to the rescue. He stood watch with his telescope at the crosstrees of the mast, searching the horizon for the longboat, but to no avail. The sun was almost setting, and Captain Raymond had about given up hope of finding the boat when he saw a black patch against the setting sun. It was a black silk handkerchief that Edward Cooper was bringing home as a present to his mother. He had tied it to the end of an oar as a signal, and it proved to be just the right thing to show up against the blinding sun.

After a fearful anxiety of two hours, when every minute seemed an age, Captain Raymond finally picked up the almost frozen passengers sometime after dark the evening of December 22, 1844. Landing in New York, Edward and Abram arrived with everything lost but the clothes on their backs, but they were thankful to Captain Raymond and his officers and crew. The experience deeply affected Abram. "It taught me that my life which had been miraculously rescued belonged not to me, and from that hour I gave it to the work which from that time has been in my thoughts—the welfare of my fellow-citizens."

The harrowing adventure, however, had a great advantage. It strengthened the Cooper-Hewitt friendship, and henceforth Hewitt was regarded as a member of the Cooper family. It is too incredible to contemplate how great the loss would have been to the nation had these two young men not survived. History would prove that their survival enabled the young men to make important contributions in later years to industry and politics.

The U.S. Coast Guard

It is interesting to point out that this shipwreck happened to have important results for all American seamen. According to an account given by Edward, he recalled, "When my father was in Congress he tried to pass a bill to establish the United States Coast Guard. This Bill was a Republican measure, and was in charge of James G. Blaine, the Republican leader. For some reason it met with serious opposition—so much so that Blaine felt sure he would be unable to pass it without some Democratic support. Blaine came over to my father's desk and asked him if he would be willing to support the Bill with his Democratic following, as it was not a party measure."

Abram was only too willing to help, and asked, "Where will I get time for my speech?"

Blaine answered, "I will give you my time."

Abram arose to the support of the bill, to the surprise of the Democratic colleagues, and he dramatically told the story of his shipwreck off the Jersey coast. Then he turned and asked the House, "How would you feel if you were driven on the coast, in a small boat, in December, with no one there to help you?"

The speech ended amid applause, and the bill was passed almost unanimously, thereby establishing the Coast Guard along all United States' coasts.

Cooper Hewitt & Company

After this shipwreck adventure, Edward and Abram were inseparable, and the experience apparently cemented their friendship for the remainder of their lives. Their combined intelligence, invention and shrewdness were further sealed when the two young men went into business together as the Cooper Hewitt & Company. When Abram Stevens Hewitt, acting for Peter Cooper, bought the Ringwood ironworks, it made for a shrewd investment in an area that Alden T. Cottrell called the "first large-scale development of the iron industry in the United States." With the purchase of Ringwood, the Cooper-Hewitt families forged a strong alliance in the iron business, and Cooper Hewitt & Company became the fifth-largest corporation in the United States. However, Hewitt was the hands-on manager and secured the contracts and ran the business on a daily basis.

A case concerning service to the government occurred during the Civil War, and Abram's quick action in the tale is legendary. During the campaign to open the Mississippi River, General Grant was held up by the Confederates at Fort Donelson, at the mouth of the Cumberland River, and the fort could only be reduced by heavy mortars. The mortars themselves were available, but Grant had no suitable mounts for them. Edward Ringwood recalled:

> *The head of the United States Government arsenals stated that it would take a number of months to make these mounts. So President Lincoln, who knew the urgency of the demand, wrote to Cooper Hewitt & Company, at that time the largest iron firm in the country, to see if they could get the mounts out in time. My father undertook the job at once. He put all his works at it with all the energy he possessed. He succeeded in shipping thirty of these mortar carriages in the unheard time of three weeks and the first were shipped within six days and on their way to the scene of action. Hewitt only charged for the actual cost of labor and materials. The bill for flat costs was rendered, but its payment was very much delayed and the firm could ill spare such money at that time. Hewitt went directly to Washington saw Secretary of War Stanton who gave Hewitt a note to the President. Lincoln expressed surprise that the sum should be held up, when the work had been so promptly done at no profit, and that Hewitt had accomplished what the War Department had declared impossible. The warrant was sent for and he wrote across it, Pay this bill now. A Lincoln.*

Not content with that, Lincoln added, "Now Mr. Stanton, I want you to do me a service. I am going to trouble you to go to the Treasury Department with Mr. Hewitt and see this bill through the proper channels for immediate payment."

Cooper Hewitt & Company fulfilled many other government contracts, including all the beams for the U.S. Capitol Building and the Treasury Building in Washington, D.C., and it produced iron girders for many prominent buildings, including the Harper Brothers building.

After Abram read Sir Henry Bessemer's famous paper presented in 1856 about the Bessemer process of producing steel, the firm was the first to install a Bessemer converter running in the works at Phillipsburg. Later in life, Abram Hewitt, like his father-in-law, Peter Cooper, received the Bessemer Gold Medal for contributions to the advancement of the iron trade. The Bessemer process successfully produced good, cheap steel for the first time, and at that time, the Erie Railroad had large amounts of iron rails that had to be rerolled periodically. Cooper Hewitt & Company had the contract for all this work. Edward Ringwood remembered:

> *When Jay Gould secured control of the Erie Railroad, he wanted to discuss this contract with my father, who invited him to Ringwood. They talked in the parlor after dinner, while my mother sat at his side and knitted. When he went upstairs my father asked my mother what she thought of Mr. Gould. She replied that she did not trust him, and that Mr. Hewitt should have nothing to do with him in business. "Why?" he asked. "He has shifty eyes, and long flat feet, and I never trust that kind of man," his wife replied. Events soon proved that my mother was right. Cooper Hewitt Co. lost the Erie contract because Mr. Hewitt was unwilling to increase the contract price and divide half of the increase with Mr. Gould personally. My mother's intuition about people was often uncanny.*

DISPUTE AT THE IRONWORKS

Edward and Abram seem to have been imbued with the same scrupulous principles of sound and fair management that Peter Cooper had believed in and fostered all his life. Hewitt, particularly, was known to have had exceptionally good relations with his employees. One example of the company's largesse concerns disgruntled workmen. In those days, when labor was frequently exploited, the firm continued to keep workers on the payroll. One stunning example of this happened during the depression of 1873–79, when the business was conducted at a great loss of $100,000 per annum. However, despite this tremendous loss in income, Abram kept the ironworks running, even when other ironworks closed down. The unwitting employees on one occasion thought that they were entitled to a raise and brought their heated complaint to management. One can just imagine the workers trudging up from the plant armed with nothing more than their misled grievances.

Acknowledging the situation, Hewitt met the foremen and ironmongers head on and invited them to his office. He was prepared for the confrontation and had pulled out the huge record books for their examination. All the ledgers indicated that the business was running at a great loss and that, despite this loss, the payrolls had been paid at the expense of the firm. When the men learned about their error in judgment, the disgruntled representatives, with a certain degree of chagrin, withdrew, and there never was any trouble again.

Peter Cooper lived to see the day when the improvements promoted by the Cooper Hewitt firm incorporated every sign of progress in the metallurgy of iron and steel in the United States and abroad. In 1862, Abram visited England to study the making of gun barrel iron and afterward created the first American open-hearth furnace. The firm's great success, however, is largely based on Abram Hewitt's close study and prescience of the iron market.

The legacy of Abram Stevens Hewitt, the last great ironmaster, and his astute business management lives on in the history of the iron industry. In *South of the Mountains*, published by the Historical Society of Rockland County, Anne E. McCabe wrote, "He was motivated by zest of competitive activity and the pleasure it gave him to be a leader in the development of American resources rather than the desire for great wealth."

HEWITT'S DISTINGUISHED CAREER

Abram A. Hewitt's political career began in 1867 when he was appointed by President Andrew Johnson a United States scientific commissioner to visit the Paris Exposition Universelle, held in France. Hewitt distinguished himself and delivered a report, which was published by Congress, on the iron and steel trade exhibited at the exposition. He emphasized the bearing of that exhibition on the actual and prospective iron and steel industry of this country. His report was widely read and translated into several foreign languages.

Abram Hewitt's astute business sense and forays into public service also brought him into the forefront of the political arena in 1875. Hewitt held office for the first time as a representative from New York in the Forty-fourth Congress, a position he held by successive reelections for twelve years. As representative of the metropolis, his thorough knowledge of business, as well as finance, was highly valued.

Abram Hewitt took an earnest interest in everything that pertained to the city of New York and was unsparing in his endeavors to aid in its development. He secured the appropriations necessary for the deepening of the ship channels and induced the federal government to commit itself to the systematic and extensive improvement of New York Harbor.

Abram Stevens Hewitt

THE REFORM MAYOR

In 1871, Hewitt joined with his friends Samuel J. Tilden and Edward Cooper in the campaign to bring about the fall of the corrupt Tammany Hall–based Tweed Ring, led by William M. Tweed, whose misdeeds had been lampooned in the cartoons of the famous political satirist Thomas Nast. Hewitt played a prominent part in reorganizing the Democratic Party in New York that Tweed and Tammany had controlled. He ventured into elective politics in 1874 when he won the seat in the U.S. House of Representatives and served in Congress for five terms. Resigning from Congress, he accepted the nomination to become mayor of New York.

Tammany gave the party a genuine surprise by nominating Abram S. Hewitt for mayor, making Democratic union not just possible but likely. Mr. Philip Henry Dugro stood up in his delegation from the Tenth District. Before he could say a word to the convention, the floor and the galleries yelled and cheered. Hats were raised on canes, and their owners stood on their chairs and danced around while they whirled their hats. With the deafening rabble of the delegates, Dugro went to the platform and said:

> *I desire to place in nomination before this Convention as a candidate for Mayor of the city of New York a citizen whose ability, integrity, and Democracy no one can gainsay, and for the union upon whom all honest Democratic citizens of New York need no conference. I leave no one a chance to fail to recognize the strength and Democracy of this citizen. I name as candidate for Mayor of the city of New York an old, honored and respected patriarch, our fellow citizen Congressman Abram Stevens Hewitt.*

After Mr. Dugro's little speech, the motion was carried to a roar and unanimous vote. Each delegate was on his feet, and for a few moments nothing could be heard above the shouts of approval. When the noise had somewhat subsided, someone proposed three cheers for the nominee, and the enthusiastic braves, those young men in the audience, broke into another roar of applause that was only checked when Brouke Cockran rose to second the nomination, saying:

> *The best eulogy that can be written of the man I name is found in the history of the nation. He does not need any introduction to the citizens of this city or the State or the country. His name is in history and his work is recorded in the stature books of the nation. The name of our candidate places this nomination beyond all desire for office or spoils. It comes from our desire for the supremacy*

of the Democratic Party. His name in itself is a tower of strength. It will bring a calm to the troubled factions of this city like the message of peace that makes the tumult be still. It means Democratic control of the city of New York, and a broad pathway to the Presidential success in 1888. Abram S. Hewitt needs no eulogy. His name has been identified with the city of New York for over a quarter of a century. He has accumulated wealth. He has helped spread commerce on every sea and every clime, and to the building up of industries of New York his life has been devoted. He has marched on the road side by side with his workingmen to the number of 5,000, and he shared with them his prosperity as he shared with them his good when panics came.

A SURPRISE NOMINATION

A reporter from *The World* newspaper, eager to interview the candidate, found Mr. Hewitt at the residence of his brother-in-law, ex-mayor Edward Cooper, where he was staying temporarily while his own house was undergoing repairs. Hewitt was reclining on a lounge in the library conversing with Mr. Cooper and ex-police commissioner Charles F. MacLean. When told by the reporter that he had been nominated for mayor by Tammany Hall, Mr. Hewitt said, "That is certainly a very handsome action on the part of Tammany Hall, but I have heard nothing of it except from you, and it is such an astounding piece of information that I cannot help thinking there must be some mistake about it."

The reporter told him that he had just come from Tammany Hall and that there was not the slightest doubt about his nomination.

"Well," resumed Mr. Hewitt. "It is very surprising but how was done? Was it done with a hurrah?" The reporter answered that he had not waited to see how the nomination was received but rather had hurried off as soon as he had ascertained definitely that Mr. Hewitt was to be the nominee.

"Well, then," exclaimed Mr. Hewitt. "They have probably changed their minds by this time and nominated somebody else."

"Will you accept the nomination, Mr. Hewitt?" asked the reporter.

"It is a little too early for me to say anything," responded Mr. Hewitt. "I have just this moment learned of the nomination from you, and do not yet even know that it is an accomplished fact. How can I be expected to say whether or not I will accept a nomination before I am officially informed of it? It would be manifestly improper for me to do so."

"Yes," interposed ex-mayor Cooper, "it would not be proper for Mr. Hewitt to say whether he will accept the nomination until he is officially notified."

The *World* reporter asked Abram if he was not a County Democrat, but before he could answer, Edward said, "Well, now, Mr. Hewitt is not going to be interviewed. He does not mean to be discourteous, you know, but he has not yet had time even to think over the matter, and besides, until he learns of the nomination officially, it would not be proper for him to say anything."

There was joy in the County Democracy Amsterdam Club when the news of the nomination was received. "Who brought it about?" someone asked of Jude Maurice Power.

"Nobody brought it about. It was plainly spontaneous."

"What does the club think about it?" a reporter asked.

"The club is delighted. There could not have been a better nomination. Mayor Grace will be greatly pleased. It means union and victory."

"Will Mr. Hewitt accept?"

"Of course I cannot say, but I have little doubt of his acceptance. His patriotism and love of his party are too strong to permit him to refuse, and throw away this assurance of victory."

MAYOR OF THE CITY OF NEW YORK

When Abram Stevens Hewitt was elected mayor of New York City on a reform ticket in 1886, he defeated United Labor candidate Henry George and the Republican Theodore Roosevelt. His involvement turned with great urgency from industry to politics. However, Hewitt would serve only one term, which was precipitated by the enemies he garnered during his tenure.

The year 1887–88 brought new challenges and responsibilities to Mayor Hewitt during his administration. His brand of governing was going to be a sharp democratic contrast from the corruption of the Tweed ring, which had robbed the city of New York of millions of dollars. Sweeping changes through the administration for the good of the city were about to be initiated by the new mayor.

On the street, people began to react to the election. "The voters had no choice," a disgruntled orator exclaimed as he held an audience of pedestrians in the grip of his ranting on a podium in Union Square. Boasting further inside knowledge of the election, the speaker responded to an angry onlooker.

"Everyone knows it was not a contest. Hewitt was elected on the Tammany ticket only because of Tammany's fear of the opposing candidates, the United Labor Party candidate, the political economist, Henry George and his single tax philosophy and Theodore Roosevelt who ran as the Republican Party candidate. Tammany never would have elected Mr. Hewitt mayor otherwise." Several workingmen in the crowd, objecting to the speaker's slanderous tirade, rose up their voices in resounding boos and catcalls, resulting in a free-for-all skirmish. The police dispersed the raucous bullies, and the tumult subsided.

Confronting Corruption

Abram Hewitt was well aware, even before the election, that he would inherit a city riddled with police graft, so he made plans to confront the corruption head-on with an ingenious mode of investigation. At Hewitt's personal expense of $50,000, he hired detectives in Chicago and California to privately investigate the entire police department.

A short time later, after he had assumed office, Mayor Hewitt called in all the high-ranking heads of the police department to his office. After the formalities of greeting everyone who had been summoned to attend the meeting, Mr. Hewitt made an announcement.

"Gentlemen," Mr. Hewitt began in a strong and commanding tone, "I am ordering you to close the gambling houses and places of ill fame. We need to clean up New York City and restore it to its rightful ownership as a reputable place for its citizens and visitors."

With guarded remarks, the police chief assured Mayor Hewitt that the cleanup would be done, and the men left the meeting. However, as they descended the front stairs of the mayor's office, they grumbled epitaphs of disrespect, and one of the police chiefs remarked, "Don't mind him at all, doesn't matter, with Hewitt as the new Tammany mayor, these orders are just window dressing for the public."

After a week when nothing had been done, Mayor Hewitt ordered all the captains of police and heads of the departments to meet him at his house at 9 Lexington Avenue, taking them into his study. Edward remembered, "They were all assembled in father's large library and father went over and locked the door. Then he asked the Chief of Police, 'Why have you not executed my orders?'"

The chief of police gave an evasive answer, to which Mayor Hewitt demanded, "Why not?" The chief then replied, "We're able to do it Mayor Hewitt, but if we put your orders into effect, your political career would be at an end."

Hewitt hotly responded, "That is none of your business, and has nothing to do with the subject in hand. I intend to have my orders executed as given, and not as interpreted by graft and politics."

Edward witnessed the most damning evidence that Mayor Hewitt had accumulated. "Mayor Hewitt took the Police Chief and department heads by surprise. He drew from his pocket the reports obtained by him from his private detectives on all the activities of the police force, and announced that he had enough evidence to send them all to Sing Sing for life."

Mayor Hewitt had read only three inflammatory reports when the chief of police interrupted, saying, "Mayor Hewitt, what do you intend to do with this information?"

Edward recalled his father saying, "I intend to keep it in my safe, so that whenever my orders are not executed properly these incriminating documents can be used by the District Attorney."

The chief of police responded to the threat of exposure by saying, "Mayor Hewitt, I believe that I can speak for all of the police captains and I assure you that your orders will be executed properly as long as you are Mayor."

Then the chief of police added one final declarative remark. "With these documents in your hands Mayor Hewitt, we will follow your orders, but you realize that your term will be a short one." This statement did not unnerve Mayor Hewitt. He knew that he had the upper hand and that the legal action that he could enact against the police department would result in a major overhauling of the corrupt operations in the city that were rampant at the time.

The very next day, the entire police department engaged in a massive cleanup and closing of vice and gambling places in a sweep like New York had never known.

THE ONE-TIME REFORM MAYOR

During Mayor Hewitt's administration, he was able to control the police force with no further application of pressure. The police were always agreeable to everything he wanted, and no one ever knew where he got his power in the Tammany administration. However, the police chief's warning, "Your term will be a short one," was realized. Hewitt was badly defeated at the next election.

During his term in office, Hewitt remained deeply involved in New York City's landmark occasions. He had served as director of the executive committee of the Brooklyn Bridge Company and is remembered for his most famous speech at the opening ceremonies in 1883. The city celebrated with great fanfare and fireworks, and the huge crowds demonstrated the enthusiasm felt by New Yorkers and Brooklynites for the city's newest monumental wonder.

He also concentrated on major municipal improvements in the city. He was noted for his public spirit and is best known for planning and financing the construction of the New York subway system. By the 1890s, new elevated lines were being used extensively by the city's prosperous middle and upper classes on the way to and from their businesses. Hewitt is rightfully recognized as the father of the New York subway system.

He also formed the plan of having small parks constructed within New York City over a long period of years. His scheme was to have the legislature pass a law to set aside certain sums of money yearly and devised his plan so that the project could not be sidetracked as soon as the Tammany politicians succeeded in electing a mayor who would do as they wanted. Tammany was opposed to the Small Parks Bill, and Hewitt was informed that Governor David Bennett Hill was also going to veto it. However, Hewitt obtained some incriminating checks that might not have been graft but looked like it. He used this information and sent a telegram to the governor noting that he wished to see a representative at Ringwood, on Sunday, without fail, on most important business for the governor. When Mr. Rice, Governor Hill's secretary, was shown into Hewitt's study, Hewitt laid out four $50,000 checks on the table. Rice looked at the governor's endorsement and then asked Hewitt what he wished the governor to do for him. Hewitt replied, "All I want, at present, was for the Governor to sign the Small Parks Bill." Needless to say, the Small Parks Bill was signed next day, and New York City got its small parks.

Some of Hewitt's mayoral decisions did not go over without some derision. In the heat of argument, Hewitt's strong resolve was challenged when he angered some New Yorkers by breaking with tradition and refusing to take a place in the reviewing stand at the St. Patrick's Day parade and also refusing to raise the flag of Ireland over City Hall on St. Patrick's Day. He argued, "The seat of the city government should represent all citizens and not a particular group or nationality." In the heavily Irish city, this decision proved unpopular and contributed to Hewitt's defeat for reelection in 1888.

Much to his credit, Hewitt was considered a consistent defender of sound money practices and civil service reform. He is famously quoted as saying, "Unnecessary taxation is unjust taxation." His groundbreaking reforms and his intolerance of partisanship made enemies within his own party. It produced an open break with Tammany Hall and led to his retirement from politics. No task had been too great, and his benevolent interest in New York City never wavered. He is remembered as "America's foremost private citizen."

NOT QUITE RETIRED

After his retirement from politics, Hewitt never quite left the public scene and instead devoted his energies elsewhere. He was a trustee of Columbia University, chairman of the board of trustees of Barnard College and one of the original trustees of the Carnegie Institution. In 1876 and again in 1890, he served as president of the American Institute of Mining Engineers. A man of his time, Abram Stevens Hewitt was one of the most noteworthy and productive North Rockland natives in history, and his philanthropy is legendary.

Other men like Hewitt who had achieved great success in life sought his counsel. Inspired by Hewitt's example of philanthropy, John Masterson Burke, who had amassed a large fortune, came to Hewitt for advice. Hewitt pondered the best consideration for Burke's money and suggested that he might endow a hospital, a convalescent home for the poor. This proposal appealed to Burke, and he subsequently left money in his will for it—with the home to be named the Winifred Masterson Burke Relief Foundation in honor of his mother. The foundation opened its doors in 1915 and operates today as the Burke Rehabilitation Hospital in White Plains, New York.

ABRAM AND AMELIA'S ENGAGEMENT

Abram Hewitt's closely entwined connection with the lifestyle of the Cooper family probably took on its strongest possible association just eight years after he was the acknowledged executive head of Cooper Hewitt

Abram Hewitt. *Courtesy of the Library of Congress.*

& Company. He had accumulated a comfortable fortune worth at least $175,000, a considerable accumulation of wealth in those days.

Peter Cooper's daughter, Amelia, was a gangly teenager when Abram first saw her, and it is no wonder that he took no particular notice of her, nor she of him. However, by the time Abram had ensconced himself in the good graces of the Cooper family, things had taken a turn of quite a different nature when it came to Amelia. By 1847, she had blossomed into a beautiful, statuesque young woman with strong features and auburn hair that framed a clear complexion and pleasant countenance. Although she attracted many suitors, she was in no hurry to get married.

COURTING AMELIA

Abram bore his short stature with upstanding dignity that befitted his exalted position as a successful businessman. Even President Lincoln had been impressed with Hewitt. "He received me with great cordiality and said, looking me up and down from head to foot, 'You are not such a hell of a big man after all. I thought from the way you made those mortar carriages that you must be at least ten feet tall.'" Well, Abram was a larger-than-life individual, and when it came to visiting Amelia, he dressed in carefully chosen Sunday attire. Whenever he visited the Cooper mansion, he wore a blue cutaway coat, black satin waistcoat and tight doeskin trousers. In this fashion, he cut a handsome figure of a man whose snappy gray eyes focused its affections on courting the lovely Amelia.

However, Abram had to be patient and establish his ascendancy as the leading contender for her hand in marriage. His credentials bestowed on him the rank of the top suitor; at least, one can ascertain this was the case in Peter Cooper's evaluation. With impressive business and financial credentials, among Amelia's suitors, Abram stood firmly on his own two feet and could be considered a good catch.

Meanwhile, Amelia enjoyed the flirtations and admiration of a string of persistent admirers. However, being on such intimate terms with the Cooper family, Abram had the advantage of paterfamilias on his side. He took pleasure in writing to the family circle and particularly to the twenty-year-old daughter who was his heart's desire.

In 1849 or thereabouts, Peter Cooper had taken his wife and Amelia to Schooley's Mountain in New Jersey to escape the heat of midsummer. Abram, on the other hand, like other businessmen, stayed in the city, but he kept as close a contact as possible with the Cooper circle. The separation did not deter Hewitt's pursuit and ardor for Cooper's only daughter. During that summer, Abram relied on correspondence to keep informed and in touch with Amelia. In letters to Abram from the Cooper family, their fondness for the young man was expressed in intimate terms, and they always sent their love expressed as follows: "So fond and pure that my black ink refuses to record all its fervor." Attempting to establish a closer connection with Amelia with gift giving of an intimate nature, in a response letter Abram wrote, "Please say to Amelia that I send up by Mr. Bishop a pair of slippers that will fit to a charm."

Abram, however, continued to find Amelia's suitors distressingly numerous. Not to be discouraged, he was assured in another letter from the Cooper circle, perhaps in this instance from her mother: "Amelia says she will send her own love, as soon as she gets a letter from you for herself. Plenty of beaus as usual. Bowley was here both Saturday and Sunday (6 hours), but don't be frightened. She understands what she is about. It amuses me to see the way Peter Cooper receives Mr. Bowley, in a way so foreign to his kindly manner. You know how hospitable and habitually friendly he is to everybody. His stiffness to Bowley is therefore more comical." It appears obvious that Peter Cooper gave Bowley the cold shoulder, most likely to exercise his preference for Abram.

Perhaps these letters from the Cooper circle gave Abram some comfort that Amelia's parents sided with his attempts to impress and woo the lovely Amelia. His prime advantage was his close business and personal relationship with the Cooper family, which created the perfect environment for him to become more attached to Amelia and fall in love. Amelia, on the other hand, had other things on her mind; she was not in any rush to accept his advances and continued to keep Abram waiting.

AMELIA'S PERSONALITY

Amelia had been brought up in wealth, albeit a somewhat somber kind, but on any occasion, she was fashionably attired in the style of a society debutante. She might have worn a gown from the Paris-based House of Worth, the renowned French couturier that excelled in creating garments with exquisite fabrics and ornamentation.

However, despite Amelia's inherited advantages, she did not become a frivolous female because her father, Peter Cooper, was a man of practical sensibilities. He believed that his children, and later his grandchildren, should each learn a trade so that if they lost everything they would still have it as a resource. Amelia had been taught housekeeping and could wash, cook and sew with the best. For a time, she attended the select classes of Mrs. Meer, at Tenth and Broadway, and while there she witnessed the erection of Grace Church underway at Tenth Street and Fourth Avenue. Groomed as a fine lady of the day, she acquired knowledge of the fine arts, and occasionally she was sent down to Howard Street to take dancing lessons given by Mr. Ferrero, an Italian patriot who had fled his country after the revolt of 1838. She finished her education at Miss Kirkland's and acquired a keen sensibility and intelligence, character qualities that transcended her attractiveness and no doubt captivated Abram's admiration and love.

Amelia was not without a vein of coquetry and knew enough to keep Hewitt in suspense. In fact, she used to tell her children, "I never was quite certain I would marry him, till I walked down the aisle to the altar." Just when Abram and Amelia became engaged has been attributed to the year

1850 or soon afterward. Furthermore, financially Abram was completely independent, and that was an essential factor in marriage standards of the day. From the moment of the engagement, Abram virtually became Peter Cooper's second son, and his dependence on Abram grew substantially.

It is curious to also note that Peter Cooper dictated certain requirements regarding the union of his daughter with Abram. The wife of a Hewitt descendant, Mrs. Robert Hewitt Stanwood Jr., who has some intimate knowledge on the subject, remembered that Peter Cooper demanded that he would also reside in any home where the couple lived. Alas, this came about when the two families lived together in Cooper's huge house at 9 Lexington Avenue. However, most indicative of Cooper's strong hold was his other stipulation that on any business enterprise or invention, the name "Peter Cooper" would be listed first. This gives credence to consider that not all of the works attributed solely to Peter Cooper were of his own creation. Case in point, Peter Cooper established Cooper Union, but it was Abram Stevens Hewitt who ran it and made it into a successful college. It was Abram who endorsed and encouraged his daughters, Amy, Sarah and Eleanor, to establish The Cooper Union Museum for the Arts of Decoration at Cooper Union. In other words, Peter Cooper was the great visionary, but it was Abram Steven Hewitt's intellect and drive that fulfilled many of the great man's ideas.

THE COOPER-HEWITT WEDDING

Abram had been a patient suitor for several years before the couple's marriage took place. Their wedding was in keeping with the simplicity characteristic of both families. Though a daughter of a millionaire, Amelia was nonetheless wed with no fanfare. In keeping with Peter Cooper's lifelong attitude of austerity, the marriage was held on April 6, 1855, at the stately Cooper house at 9 Lexington Avenue when Amelia was twenty-five and Abram thirty-three years old. There they lived their entire lives, except for the summer months and winter holidays at Ringwood. Reverend Henry Whitney Bellows of All Souls Unitarian Church, located at the time at Twentieth Street and Fourth Avenue, where the Coopers worshipped, performed the ceremony.

In this domestic setting, Amelia's wedding was celebrated with a modest wedding dinner with their immediate families. Despite the austerity of

This page: 9 Lexington Avenue.
Courtesy of the Library of Congress,
Historic American Buildings Survey.

this marriage, it would not become the paradigm for the marriages of their offspring, whose marriages would subsequently become more lavish and newsworthy.

It was fortuitous that Abram married Amelia, as this alliance enabled Hewitt to forge a partnership with Peter Cooper that became more than a mere relationship between in-laws. Hewitt seemed to be cut from the same cloth as Cooper and possessed the same knack for invention and mechanics and the same wide interests and acts of benevolence that mirrored the honesty, invention, sturdy independence and self-reliance of his father-in-law. As a result, in later years Peter Cooper began to rely more heavily on Abram's alert intelligence in business and family matters.

A COOPER HOUSEHOLD

The Cooper household's no-frills decoration reflected Peter Cooper's austere outlook. Emily Post, the noted arbiter of etiquette and a resident of Tuxedo Park, described it best in the following dedication "To Miss Sarah Hewitt and Miss Eleanor Hewitt, with the sincere affection of Emily Post." Under the subject "Cards and Visits," she referred to the Cooper house near Gramercy Park:

> There are a few old-fashioned ladies, living in old-fashioned houses, and still staying at home in the old-fashioned way to old-fashioned friends who for decades have dropped in for a cup of tea and a chat. And there are two maiden ladies in particular, joint chatelaines of an imposing beautiful old house where, on a certain afternoon of the week, if you come in for tea, you are sure to meet not alone those prominent in the world of fashion, but a fair admixture of artists, scientists, authors, inventors, distinguished strangers—in a word Best Society in its truest sense. But days at home such as these are not easily duplicated; for few houses possess a "salon" atmosphere, and few hostesses achieve either the social talent or the wide cultivation necessary to attract and interest so varied and brilliant a company.

Post's description pretty much sums up the lifestyle under Cooper's rule.

THE HOUSE TRANSFORMATION

The Hewitts both loved to entertain, and once the family became the sole occupants of 9 Lexington Avenue, they made hospitality plans high on their social agenda. It is not surprising, therefore, that a year or two after Cooper's death in 1883, the Hewitts had the house remodeled by the young architect Stanford White of McKim, Mead and White, the leading architects of the day.

From the point of view of Mrs. Hewitt and her daughters, White was the logical choice for the job as he worked very much in the Beaux Arts manner, converting the mid-Victorian mansion into a stately English townhouse. Mr. Hewitt made an Italian palace of the old Cooper mansion and introduced the kind of luxury that Peter Cooper had always eschewed. The wide front step stoop was removed, and a new modern ground-floor entrance was created. The Hewitts and their guests entered the house through a portal of Doric columns, and the glass panel door was etched with the number "9" gilded in gold. A section of the lower floor was also made over into a large, book-lined study for Mr. Hewitt.

Stanford White's penchant for marble dominated the interior. Marble was everywhere, from the entrance to the reception room at the right and the big reception room at the left for ladies. The marble staircase was ornamental and bedecked with thick, tasseled red ropes hung from the balustrades. The staircase led up to a fine open vista, around which were the various salons and dining room.

The transformation of the Cooper mansion was extravagant, but it suited the Hewitts' lifestyle. The second floor contained the "blue library," the "green parlor" and the "red drawing room," where Mrs. Hewitt used to serve tea every afternoon. The green and red rooms were furnished in the styles of Louis XV and Louis XVI and represented Sarah Cooper's French taste.

The dramatic scene of many lively fancy dress entertainments and receptions were held in the Hewitts' music room, which looked out on a large courtyard where the greenhouse used to be located. The dining room on the same floor, in the style of acquired splendor, had a decorative Moorish ceiling with the dramatic sweep of an allegorical mural that covered most of the room just below the ceiling. Mr. and Mrs. Hewitt, on one of their European trips, had obtained the mural from a Venetian palace on the Grand Canal in Venice, Italy, and they believed it was a Tintoretto. Confronted by such ostentation, as well as the marble, the mural and the red velvet, one may justifiably wonder what old Peter Cooper would have thought about the transformation of the formerly austere interior. With such a stately mansion at their disposal, the Hewitts' home became the epicenter of some of the most celebrated events. To be invited to their mansion was highly desired by a diverse cross-section of people who were themselves counted among the upper echelons of society.

A Housewarming Party

To celebrate the unveiling of the elaborate renovations, the Hewitts gave a housewarming party at their residence on Lexington Avenue. The transformation of the house, which Peter Cooper had built in the 1850s, converted a plain Victorian double brownstone into a graceful Georgian townhouse, and Mayor Hewitt seemed particularly delighted to show it off.

The guests were the members of families who defined society of the day and included Bessy Marbury, a great friend of Sarah Cooper Hewitt's, along with a contingent of Roosevelts, Fishes, Harrimans, Jays and Schermerhorns. Elsie de Wolfe, Lady Mendl, who lived nearby, also participated in the festivities, which included an afternoon entertainment provided by the Hewitt sisters' Ladies Amateur Orchestra. Now that the Hewitt house was officially launched, and with an outlook of prosperity and society, many other forms of entertainment—including dinner parties and festive, fancy dress balls—took place there.

The Fabled Costume Party

Abram and his wife fully endorsed the entertainments, and the Hewitt sisters, like other young women of their social strata, willingly engaged in the Gilded Age tradition of fabulous, frivolous costume parties. The newspapers responded in their society columns with detailed reports of the festivities. "One of the most amusing entertainments in many years was given by Misses Sarah and Eleanor Hewitt at the residence of their parents at 9 Lexington Avenue last evening," reported the *New York Times* concerning a costume event that took place on the evening of April 6, 1899. "An element of New York society, in which the Misses Hewitts are prominent, has found its chief pleasure in the organization and carrying over of clever costume suppers and dances." Describing the previous year's event, the newspaper added, "Last year the Misses Hewitts devised the scheme of a vegetable and flower party. Their guests impersonated familiar garden flowers and vegetables. This year the young women hit upon the idea of a travesty on operatic and musical events of the past season."

You can well imagine the high drama and fascination a bewildered onlooker might have had as he viewed the arrival of the costumed guests at 9 Lexington Avenue. The newspaper account further described the entourage:

Nearly 150 men and women, who had entered into the spirit of the affair, had assembled at the Hewitt mansion. They had arranged themselves in some phantasmagorical costume as to convey the idea that they represented some musical event or incident, character or work. As they entered the door the guests passed to the rear of the parlors, which extended the whole length of the house. Each guest was supposed to walk down the aisle performing some instrument, or so acting carrying out the character assumed, until reaching the west end of the parlour where ex-Mayor and Mrs. Hewitt stood to receive them. According to the newspaper account Mr. and Mrs. Peter Barlow the essence of French comic opera were among the best characters. Mr. Edward Valpy, who towered over the other performers in the procession, portrayed a Scotch piper in a very original and amusing costume. His kilt was dark green and blue plaid, his jacket scarlet on which was pinned a great medal with the legend, "I am hungry." His blaring red beard and wig with a Glengarry bonnet on his head completed the impersonation. Under his arm he carried a Scottish Highland bagpipe on which he executed mournful pibrochs to the applause and laughter of the crowd.

The chorus of nuns and monks paraded in succession with society ladies in disguise including Mrs. Henry G. Trevor, Miss Sarah Hewitt, Miss Alice Van Rensselaer and Miss Eleanor Garnier Hewitt among the pious impersonators.

A great deal of preparation and practice must have gone into the theatrical ensembles. A band of Negro Minstrels in full makeup excited much amusement especially when they performed a "cake walk" and the delighted onlookers responded enthusiastically, now and then, when they sang familiar "coon songs."

Mrs. Stanford White, the wife of the noted architect Samuel White of the noted firm McKim & White was another reveler. The "Song of Nations" was under the leadership of Mrs. White, who impersonated "Hail Columbia." Wearing a red, white and blue gown, the costume completed by a Liberty cap, she made a striking figure as she led the procession of the countries as they paraded before the group singing the "The Star Spangled Banner." A number of guests wore Louis XIV costumes and some men came as Turks. Other guests representing Little Bo Peep, Mary Had a Little Lamb and Old Mother Hubbard were also most laughable. So what does society do after such an entertaining parade? After supper was served informal dancing rounded out the evening's festivities to the strains of a stringed orchestra.

When they weren't engaged in these outlandish festivities, the members of the Hewitt household welcomed a lively mix of guests. During the social season in New York, when they were not at Ringwood, the Hewitts entertained in the Venetian dining room for a cast of more than thirty of their intimate friends, acquaintances and foreign visitors, who usually came with a letter of introduction. It was a place to be seen and to meet people from a wide mix from the political, scientific and artistic pillars of society. In typical Victorian style, meals often had twelve courses, with a complement of different utensils and excellent wines to accompany each serving.

THE HEWITT FAMILY

The Hewitt household was a lively place, and children dominated the domestic and social scene. All of Amelia and Abram's children were born at 9 Lexington Avenue except Erskine, who was born at Ringwood Manor. Sarah Cooper and Eleanor Garnier never married and obviously preferred it that way.

Concerning Sarah and Eleanor's desire to remain single, Edward Ringwood recalled how it came about that two stuffed peacocks were perched on the marble balustrades along the wide marble staircase connecting the first and second floors of their home at 9 Lexington Avenue: "They were presented, alive, to Abram Hewitt by Morris K, Jessup, a man who was also fond of peacocks and an early president of the American Museum of Natural History. Mr. Hewitt promptly put them on his lawn at Ringwood. Early the next morning the peacocks made such a terrific noise squealing that Hewitt ordered Edward to shoot them." He did this with pleasure. Mr. Hewitt then had them stuffed for display. Edward said, "The theory used to be that if you had peacocks around, you didn't get married, so my sisters, who preferred their single freedom, had them put in their New York residence to guard against any encroaching male suitors."

THE HEWITT MEN

Of the Hewitt men, Peter Cooper Hewitt most lived up to the old adage that "the apple doesn't fall far from the tree." He was always inventing, tinkering and tampering, and he started his career as an inventor in the old greenhouse attached to the house at 9 Lexington Avenue that his grandfather, Peter Cooper, had fixed up as a workshop for his grandsons.

Peter Cooper's namesake became a respected inventor himself and spent much of his adult life devoted to scientific experimentation and investigation. Peter Cooper received a patent for his invention of the

"Cooper Hewitt Mercury-Vapor Lamp," which is a direct antecedent of modern florescent lighting. There became a great demand for the product, and Hewitt and George Westinghouse formed the Cooper Hewitt Electric Company to manufacture

Peter Cooper Hewitt. *Courtesy of the Library of Congress.*

Mrs. Peter Cooper
Hewitt, "Bundle Day,"
New York, February
14, 1915. *Courtesy of the
Library of Congress.*

and sell the new lamps. The enterprise was later bought out by the
General Electric Company.

In time, Hewitt turned his passion to the development of a small hydroplane
boat and received patents to build a helicopter with Francis B. Crocker. Together
they constructed a full-size working example, and this is where the life of the
modern helicopter began for the United States Army. Hewitt predicted that one
day, aircraft would be more plentiful and cheaper than automobiles.

In 1887, Peter Cooper Hewitt married Lucy Bond Work, daughter of
New York dry goods merchant and banker Frank Work. There is some
royal connection to this union. Lucy Bond Work was the sister of Frances
Ellen Work, and Frances was the great-grandmother of the late Diana,
Princess of Wales. No children are recorded from the Hewitt/Work
marriage. They were divorced in 1918.

Then came into this prominent, highly respected and successful family one Maryon Denning, the former Maryon Brugiere (née Jeanne Andrews). A striking beauty and several times married divorcee, she had fervent aspirations to be rich and to be a part of high society. Like a romance right out of the pages of a soap opera, Maryon the opportunist met the wealthy industrialist Peter Cooper Hewitt and carried on an illicit affair, resulting in the birth of Ann Cooper Hewitt in 1914. Hewitt and Maryon eventually married in 1918, legalizing Ann as a rightful Hewitt heir. This was fortuitous for Ann because, sadly, Peter Cooper Hewitt died in 1921 after a failed appendectomy operation while he was in Paris.

Though the scandalous case of Ann Cooper Hewitt is barely remembered today, it is sufficient to mention that the arrangement of Peter Cooper Hewitt's estate concerned a trust fund. It would become the subject of much speculation when daughter Ann, the heiress to a Hewitt fortune, brought suit against her mother, who coveted a large share of a rather substantial inheritance by dubious means. It was a sensational scandal because when Ann was twenty and still technically a minor, she was the unknowing recipient of a salpingectomy (removal of a Fallopian tube), undertaken at the request of her mother. The case caught the attention of San Francisco district attorney's office, which soon announced plans to charge doctors Tilton Tillman and Samuel Boyd, as well as Maryon Cooper Hewitt, with the felony of "mayhem" for performing the procedure because of Ann's "feeblemindedness," which was later disproved. In the end, Ann refused to testify against her mother, and without Ann's testimony, the district attorney had no choice but to drop the case. Ann decided to settle her $500,000 civil case against Maryon for the sum of $150,000. So ended the legal proceedings. Ann got on with her life and—like mother like daughter—married and divorced five times. She died in 1956 at the age of forty.

EDWARD RINGWOOD HEWITT

The Hewitt sons were born inventors and often collaborated together. Edward Ringwood and Peter Cooper worked in conjunction with the invention of the Mack (a six-wheel truck), and an engine of Edward's powered the Mack truck for a number of years. In competing with the Wright brothers in aviation,

An exterior view of Ringwood Manor. *Courtesy of the Library of Congress, Historic American Buildings Survey.*

Another view from outside Ringwood Manor. *Courtesy of the Library of Congress, Historic American Buildings Survey.*

Edward Hewitt unsuccessfully tried to fly from the building that stands on Cooper Union property now; he landed in an apple tree and broke his arm. Most significantly, Edward Ringwood was an extremely knowledgeable and innovative angler, fly-fishing author, inventor, engineer and conservationist. He bought 2,700 acres, including four miles of the stream in Neversink watershed, in 1918 and established a trout laboratory. By the 1930s, he was the country's leading authority on trout stream improvement techniques.

An author of considerable note, Edward Ringwood Hewitt wrote several books, among which *A Trout and Salmon Fisherman for 75 Years* (Scribners, 1948) combines Hewitt's two earlier books, both now classics on the subject: *Telling on the Trout* and *Secrets of the Salmon*. The account of his family and their days spent in Ringwood Manor in Ringwood, New Jersey, is lovingly told in the book *Ringwood Manor: The Home of the Hewitts* (1946), dedicated to his mother.

In his nostalgic book, *Those Were the Days: Tales of a Long Life* (1943), Hewitt described the great blizzard of 1888, during which 20.9 inches of snow fell on New York, totally paralyzing the city between March 12 and March 14:

> *I was in college at Princeton, but I happened to be home that weekend. The next day the snow on Lexington Avenue was six to eight feet deep. They had to make tunnels in some places where the drifts were very high. There was one on the corner of East Twenty-first Street and Lexington Avenue. I went uptown on Broadway and Fifth Avenue. The shops had signs on them saying: "Will reopen when the flowers bloom in spring." It took New York over a week to dig itself out.*

The storm severely damaged telephone and telegraph lines, and plans (which Mayor Hewitt promoted) were speeded up to install such wires underground.

Hewitt dedicated *Those Were the Days* to his wife, Mary Emma Ashley, the daughter of James Mitchell Ashley of Toledo, Ohio, ex-governor of the Territory of Montana (1869–70) and president of the Toledo, Ann Arbor & North Michigan Railroad.

EDWARD RINGWOOD AND MARY EMMA ASHLEY

Edward and Mary Emma met while students in Berlin, Germany. In the summer of 1889, Miss Ashley, a graduate of the University of Pennsylvania, sought Berlin to perfect her understanding of the German language. Edward was pursuing a course in chemistry when the bright and pretty Ohio girl caught his eye.

In the meantime, however, in Edward Ringwood's desire to succeed in the world of business and invention and to live up to the standards set by his grandfather, Peter Cooper, he made an unusual decision. "Old News," the *Ann Arbor Argus*, reported on September 9, 1892:

> *When Mr. Hewitt visited England some time ago it was as the guest of the duke of Marlborough. On relinquishing that nobleman's hospitality the young American sought Chatham, where, donning the garb of a mechanic he enrolled himself among the mill hands. He had not been there long, however, when he was recognized by titled visitors to the famous mills of Chatham as the duke of Marlborough's guest. "Ah really, we thought you were a gentleman," remarked an astonished aristocrat, leveling his monocle at the grimy laborer, his former companion at the duke's table.' To his affront Peter Cooper's grandson replied, "I would rather be an American master mechanic than an English gentleman."*

THE YOUNG COUPLE

The romance between Mary Emma Ashley and Edward Ringwood Hewitt took its usual course of courtship, and they were married in 1892 in a rather simple ceremony. The *Detroit Evening News* recorded the following account of the wedding:

> *A romance, involving higher education and varied social interests resulted in a wedding today at Monroe cottage, Put-in-Bay, Lake Erie. Monroe cottage is the summer home of ex-Governor James M. Ashley, of Toledo, president of the Toledo, Ann Arbor & North Michigan railroad, and well known in the financial worlds of Boston and New York.*
>
> *At high noon, in the pleasant summer nook, and encircled by the family's closest friends, Miss Mary Emma Ashley, the governor's only daughter, plighted her troth to Edward Ringwood Hewitt, son of ex-mayor Abram S. Hewitt, of New York, and the favorite grandson of the late Peter Cooper.*
>
> *The wedding was in keeping with the simplicity characteristic of both families. There was neither a bridesmaid nor best man. The wedding ring was made by Edward Ringwood himself from a $10 gold piece given to him by his grandfather, Peter Cooper, as a reward for his first boyish*

evidence of mechanical skill. Hewitt's gift to his bride was a large amethyst heart incrusted in diamonds and surmounted with a crown.

The young couple would become the darlings of New York society and were the parents of sons Ashley and Abram Stevens Hewitt II and daughters Lucy and Candace.

Erskine Hewitt

While two sons took science and industry for their province, Erskine Hewitt, the last of the Hewitts to live at Ringwood, like his forebearers was a philanthropist, author and business executive whose interest was deeply rooted in history. His name, Erskine, appropriately harkens back to the Revolutionary War hero and Ringwood ironmaster Robert Erskine. The youngest Hewitt child and the only Hewitt born at Ringwood, Erskine still did not have a name by the time he was almost four years old, and this started a violent family discussion. Reverend Dr. Thomas M. Peters, who came up to Ringwood twice during each summer to conduct services in the schoolhouse and christen the children, lost patience, put on his robe, stood up and said, "As you have failed to find any name I will christen him Erskine after the tombstone in the graveyard which I passed on my way from the schoolhouse."

Erskine lived at Ringwood almost his entire life and authored a booklet, *The Forges and Manor of Ringwood*, based on his personal appreciation of the historical integrity of the place. He distinguished himself in his military career and served in Puerto Rico during the Spanish-American War. As a captain, he served as assistant adjunct on General H. Wilson's staff.

Erskine's business associations were many and included the Cooper Hewitt & Company, New Jersey Steel, Trenton Iron Works and the Ringwood Company. Like his brothers, he was a leader, an officer or director of many corporations, including IBM.

Fortunately for the Cooper-Hewitt dynasty of New York, Erskine was deeply interested in history. He restored Ringwood Manor; established a collection of Americana; collected documents, manuscripts and prints; and donated Ringwood Manor and its surrounding acreage to the State of New Jersey in 1936, with the land to be maintained as the Ringwood Manor,

Ringwood State Park. The area including the manor house was declared a National Historic Landmark District in 1966.

SOME HISTORICAL ACCOUNT OF RINGWOOD

The saga of the Cooper-Hewitt dynasty would not be complete without some account of Ringwood, for the families profited from its mines. The Hewitts were great keepers of the histories of colonial ironmasters, as well as the Forges and Manor, and they kept alive Ringwood's importance. Their sense of patriotism ran deep throughout their lives, and they were proud of it. Located in northern Passaic County, New Jersey, Ringwood is without question one of New Jersey's greatest historical treasures. The Hewitts paid reverence to the history of the American Revolution and to the role of the early iron prospectors, who came to America for rich iron ore like that found in Ringwood.

Its history dates way back to the 1740s, starting with Cornelius Board and followed by the Ogdens, Peter Hasenclever, John Jacob Faesch, Robert Erskine and Martin J. Ryerson. The last large property purchase was made in 1854 by Peter Cooper and his son-in-law, Abram Stevens Hewitt.

During the American Revolution, Robert Erskine, who was General Washington's mapmaker, created more than two hundred maps for the army, which heretofore had to rely on British maps of the region that were often inaccurate. One of his maps showed some Revolutionary troop movements, with notations in General Washington's familiar hand. (The map is now part of the J.P. Morgan Library Collection in New York City.)

Erskine organized the first company of militia in northern New Jersey. Equipping them at his own expense, he bought uniforms and boots for his private army, which guarded Ringwood during the Revolution and kept the Ringwood furnaces producing the much-needed iron products for the army while also protecting the British-owned American Iron Company's interests. At Ringwood Manor, a portrait of General Washington (called *The Prayer at Valley Forge*) is a particularly touching tribute to the Continental army, which lost nearly a quarter of its forces in the winter of 1778.

The site still contains relics of the ironworks that was in operation since the time of Robert Erskine, including a trip hammer, an anvil and a Director-class mortar base that was produced by the Cooper Hewitt and Company. Some of the Civil War guns—one of each gun used during the war by

Left: The front door of Ringwood Manor. *Courtesy of the Library of Congress, Historic American Buildings Survey.*

Below: An antique cannon on the lawn of Ringwood Manor. *Courtesy of the Library of Congress, Historic American Buildings Survey.*

both the North and South, acquired from the United States government by Abram Hewitt—are also on display at Ringwood Manor.

RINGWOOD MANOR'S TRANSFORMATION

Abram and Amelia spent their first summer at Ringwood in 1857. Amelia was so delighted with the place that Abram made Ringwood his legal residence, spending the winters with Peter Cooper in New York and summers and winter holidays at Ringwood. They were drawn to Ringwood's bucolic setting and decided to make it their second home, naming it the Forges and Manor of Ringwood. However, when the Hewitts took over Ringwood, the grounds surrounding the house were in a state of unquestionable abandon and deterioration. Edward Ringwood recalled his mother's dilemma:

> When my mother came to Ringwood to live, it must have been a most unsightly place for a summer home. The old furnace had only been out of blast for nine years and the whole place was littered with the remains of an iron business, which had been in operation for over one hundred years. Slag heaps and cinder heaps and charcoal was everywhere. A small cannon and remnants of the famous chain that was stretched across the Hudson below West Point during the American Revolution, whose links had been forged in this historic region, were among the war trophies set about the place. It took more than 25 years to get the place cleaned up so that it looked like a home and not a place of business.

In an attempt to domesticate the manor house, which was a ten-room Federal building, Amelia had a formidable task of transforming it, and many of the nearby building structures were moved up and assembled into one rambling house. When the manor house of curious architecture was finally all pieced together, the question of painting it came up, as the walls of the various buildings were finished in all kinds of ways, with shingles and clapboards of all sizes. One of Hewitt's sons, Peter Cooper, suggested, "The walls should be covered in cement laid on wire netting and whitewashed." This plastering over the old house accounted for some of the queer architectural features of the outside of the house, where the pitch of the irregular roof is broken by ten gables. Later, by placing a new roof over the tops of these building, some semblance of unity was achieved. With its bay windows, gables and Ionic columns, the whole exterior of the manor house suggests the Victorian era, with ornamentation as the rule. The building's porte-cochere was designed by the eminent architect Stanford White, who was a personal friend of the Hewitt family. In contrast, the interior of the house is essentially an ambivalent mix of furniture with Victorian and early American influence.

THE RINGWOOD GARDENS

In the garden's glory days, one might find all kinds of fruits, whether on tree or bush or vine, and everywhere flowers. The area around the manor house was painstakingly fashioned into a beautiful garden, but neither Amelia nor her daughters ever had a final plan for this garden; instead they changed it many times after their numerous trips to Europe. Mrs. Hewitt once said that while she "could not paint a picture, she could create one," and indeed she did.

Placed throughout the garden was a mixture of French, Italian and English garden statues and ornaments. The gardens themselves may have been inspired by the classical designs in the Palace of Versailles, as the Hewitt women created a "jardin a la francaise." A sentimental addition was the Neapolitan copies of old Pompeian benches that had been a wedding anniversary present from Abram to his wife. In the garden's best years, an exquisite little fountain was set in a grove of locust trees with the figure of a youthful Triton blowing a conch shell. Sarah improved the vista in 1895 by creating a large pond to the west of the house, called Sally's pond. In its productive day, the greenhouse had a large variety of plants, including vines of muscatel grapes, a gift of Sir William Cunard, who had received the cuttings from the Spanish royal family when he opened a shipping route from England to Spain.

MRS. ABRAM HEWITT'S HOME

The manor house reflects the personal preferences of one of the most influential and wealthy families of the nineteenth century, who were estimated to have amassed the sixth-largest personal fortune in America. The manor had fashionably appointed interior rooms that reflected the refined taste of the family's French Huguenot ancestry. The drawing room, with its Louis XVI furnishings, was decorated in the French manner, while the carved wooden mantel is from Peter Cooper's old house in New York at Fourth Avenue and Twenty-eight Street. It was removed to Ringwood when the Cooper house in New York was torn down. This was one of the major rooms that the Cooper-Hewitts had used for formal entertaining. Intact in the house is a treasured heirloom: a table by Abram's father, master cabinetmaker John Hewitt, who was a rival of Duncan Phyfe.

The adjacent music room was one of the three rooms, along with the French drawing room and great hall, used by the Hewitt family for entertaining guests. With its plush blue upholstered furniture, it was the scene of musicales and recitals by outstanding artists who performed for the Cooper-Hewitts and their guests. Each panel of the wallpaper in the music room, ordered by Mrs. Hewitt in France, was individually hand painted with marine-themed scenes that lent a panoramic view of sailing ships on a mesmerizing blue ocean. Amelia's bedroom was decorated in the Louis XV Revival style, while another lovely bedroom with mirrored doors, adjacent to the Abram's bedroom, was used by Mr. Hewitt's personal secretary.

Of special note, the master bedroom had been redecorated—with charming rose print curtains, bed and chaise lounge slipcovers and a dressing table—as a honeymoon suite for Eleanor Margaret, the daughter of Amy Hewitt and Dr. James Olive Green, who would marry Prince Viggo of Denmark in 1924.

The impressive dining room features furnishing from the nineteenth century and was the site of many dinners (both family style and those more celebrated). It had a wood-paneled ambiance, and the dinner table with the extensions could seat twelve guests or more.

The Hewitts were avid collectors of classic art from the Hudson River School of Art, including works by Thomas Cole, Jasper F. Cropsey and James Peale. The Hewitt sisters may well have contributed to the art collection as they traveled extensively in Europe during the development of French impressionism. There is also a fine painting of Peter Cooper, painted in 1883 and attributed to John Singer Sargent, but according to officials at Ringwood State Park, the painting is signed by the society artist Gordon Stevenson, who was a pupil of John Singer Sargent. This seems logical because Gordon Stevenson was a son-in-law of Edward Ringwood, who probably commissioned the work, which was painted after a photo of Cooper.

Abram rebuilt Ringwood Manor over several years. The commodious fifty-one-room house—with twenty-eight bedrooms, twenty-four fireplaces and thirteen bathrooms—was fitted out to accommodate not only the family but also the numerous guests who visited. It was regentrified in an eclectic style typical of the Victorian period, and it was also the site of many well-dressed gatherings. Included among the social intelligentsia were friends who attended from tony Tuxedo Park nearby, a private resort that a number of financial, industrial and social leaders called home.

THE HEWITTS' TUXEDO PARK FRIENDS

Tuxedo Park, with its mansions, a clubhouse and a park, was established in 1886 by Pierre Lorillard IV, the grandson of Peter Lorillard, on the family's land. In about eighteen months, twenty miles of roads, three dams, a clubhouse and a gate, planned by Ernest Bowditch and architect Bruce Price, completed a private resort that remains inaccessible to the public today. Early members of the Tuxedo Club were Peter Cooper, John Jacob Astor, William Waldorf Astor, J.P. Morgan and William Pierson Hamilton, the great-grandson of Alexander Hamilton, who married J.P. Morgan's daughter, Julie. Augustus D. Juilliard, who endowed the music school named after him, and Paul Tuckerman, the father of Dorothy Draper and Anson Phelps Stokes, were also counted among the elite residents.

It is of interest to note that the tuxedo, worn by men today, originated at one of the organization's autumn balls when Pierre Lorillard's son, Griswold, and some of his spunky friends cut the tails off the required formalwear of the day. The short jacket shocked the society guests, as the men were "out of uniform," to say the least. The story of the short dinner jacket spread like wildfire in newspapers across the country, and the tuxedo was born. Some historians argue that the tuxedo was fashioned after a Savile Row dinner suit. Legend has it that James Brown Potter, a Tuxedo Club member, was invited by the Prince of Wales, the future king of England, to a dinner at Sandringham. Concerned about the proper protocol for attire, Potter asked the prince for his advice. The prince put Potter in touch with his own Savile Row tailor in London,

Henry Poole & Company, where he was fitted with a short black dinner jacket. Potter liked the new look so much that he brought it back to Tuxedo Park. Either way, it's an engaging story, but I much prefer the hi-jinks of the Lorillard men.

During Ringwood Manor's heyday, dressing for the occasion was de rigueur, and the Hewitt women, who made frequent trips to Paris, had a large wardrobe of gowns custom-made for them by the French couture house of Charles Frederick Worth. The varying styles of dress worn by the Hewitt sisters, who preferred to wear old-fashioned styles, ranged from crinoline to the bustle and the vast sleeves of the Gibson girl.

ROMANCE AT RINGWOOD

While the coming and goings of distinguished guests who visited Ringwood were numerous, the everyday joys of the bucolic estate gave the Hewitt boys time to play their pranks on unwitting guests, particularly the young men who courted their sister, Amy.

Edward Ringwood remembered:

> *My eldest sister, Amy, had many beaux. Some of them we liked, as they were nice to the younger children, but others were not so popular. A coon hunt was arranged for a house party, which included one man we particularly disliked, but he was unwilling to take part in it and preferred to sleep. That night we got a nineteen pound coon, which we brought home in triumph. My sister's beau was leaving in the morning, and while he was at breakfast we unpacked his bag, put his clothes in the bureau drawer and put in the coon, which was just the right weight. Next morning the following telegram arrived from Newport, Rhode Island, "Please send clothes. Coon no use for house party at Mrs. Astors." My sister did not marry this one.*

Despite their efforts to discourage Amy's suitors, she eventually became engaged and was married in grand style to a gentleman from Kentucky.

A HEWITT WEDDING

It was the social event of that time. "My sister Amy's wedding to Dr. James Olive Green of Kentucky was the largest party we ever had at Ringwood," wrote Edward in his nostalgic book *Ringwood Manor: The Home of the Hewitts.*

Invitations went out far and wide and also included a card with travel information. A special train was to leave West Twenty-third Street at half past ten o'clock in the morning. Returning, it was to leave Ringwood at four o'clock in the afternoon and reach New York at half past five o'clock in the evening. Guests were to please present the card at the ferry and to the conductor.

The manor house at Ringwood braced for the arrival of guests, and enormous effort went into the wedding preparations. It was the setting for the celebrated wedding of the only Hewitt sister to marry, and the house was taxed to the limit with guests. The wedding took place on November 15, 1886, on a crisp fall day in wonderful weather. Edward remembered the guests' arrival: "There were large numbers of visitors from Tuxedo and from all the surrounding country and in those days, before the automobile, all the local guests arrived in horse-drawn traps of various kinds." The *New York Times* article "Yesterday's Weddings," from November 16, 1886, reported further details: "Over the little branch railroad, which brings Ringwood its train once a day, came a crowded special, which left Jersey City at 10:30 o'clock, saving those who came from New York the inconvenience of rising early."

The extensive guest list included names of people recognizable from the society pages, while others were prominent in business, and there were many residents from New York and prestigious Tuxedo Park. Counted among the notables were Mr. and Mrs. Norvin Green, parents of the groom; John Jay, the ex-mayor of New York City; Mr. and Mrs. Pierre Lorillard Jr. of Tuxedo Park; Mrs. Oliver Belmont of the noted Long Island Horse breeders; Mr. and Mrs. William Rather Duncan of the Duncan Hines fortune; Mr. and Mrs. Jordan Mott; Mr. and Mrs. James Lawrence Breese; Mr. James Brown Potter; Mr. and Mrs. Barbey; and Mr. and Mrs. Richard Mortimer.

Adding to the festivities in honor of the bride's wedding day, there was a holiday in the mines. In the early morning, the miners and laborers came down from their cottages in the mines and assembled in force about the station, waiting to see the special train arrive with friends and relatives of the bride and groom.

Louis P. West, who worked on the Hewitt farm and in the mines, further described the event in his "I Remember Ringwood" series. Recalling the elaborate wedding arrangements, he wrote:

Obviously great advance plans had been made to transform the Manor House into a woodland paradise. The brothers and sisters of the young bride to be had been engaged in conducting the elaborate arrangements for the happy event, particularly Miss Sally who was here, there and everywhere. Several hundred laborers and miners in the employ of the Hewitts robbed the forest of hemlock branches, trailing vines and mosses and speedily converted them into decorations. The out buildings, barns and recently built fences were painted red and little indeed escaped the painter's brush. Even the pig pen assumed a deep rosy hue. The pigs grunting along and rubbing themselves against the newly painted fences, assumed the color of boiled lobsters.

Inside the manor house, everything was in pristine condition. The great parlor in which the ceremony was performed was handsomely decorated, and the waxed floor was covered in the center with a huge Turkish rug. On the walls hung enormous pieces of quaint and ancient tapestry representing country scenes and knights and dames of the age of chivalry.

The effort to create an outdoor ambiance within the rooms was done with massive floral decorations. The great bay window was adorned with flowers and vines and the pillars were ivy-clad; the sides were sprinkled with La France roses. A proliferation of rhododendron adorned the foot of the walls, and there were pots of chrysanthemums and huge bunches of American Beauty that decorated the mantel. All of the rare plants, handsome cut flowers and twining evergreens from the Ringwood grounds were created on a magnificent scale and concealed the walls, were hung from the ceilings, were twined about the stairway and were brought together by festoons of pink silk ribbon.

It was the wedding of the season, and the society columns in the newspapers gave ample space to the details. The *New York Times'* "Yesterday's Weddings" column reported:

Into this beautiful floral and picturesque autumn leaves setting the guests assembled to witness the ceremony, which by invitation was stated to be held "at half past twelve o'clock," but due to the great number of people involved and the setting up it was held at one o'clock.

In the large hall Mr. and Mrs. Hewitt received the multitude of guests. Broad white ribbons cordoned off an aisle through which the bridal party could pass. The tension mounted as guests waited, then the strains of the wedding march filled the huge house and the bridal party descended the stairway. It entered the room headed by the ushers, Mr. Peter Cooper Hewitt and Mr. Edward Ringwood Hewitt, the bride's brothers, followed by Mr. F. Gray Griswold, Mr. Center Hitchcock, Mr. Charles G. Peters and Mr. Griswold Lorillard. The bridesmaids who preceded the bride were her sisters, Miss Sarah Cooper Hewitt and Miss Eleanor Garnier Hewitt. Little Clare and Leila Bryce, the daughters of Edith Cooper and Lloyd Stephens Bryce, were flower girls. They wore pretty little white gowns with pink ribbons and sashes, and carried pink roses.

At the bay window the bridegroom stood, attended by his best man, Mr. Allen Throndyke Rice. All eyes turned to the bride, leaning on her father's arm. Amy was a tall, slim brunette with dark soft eyes. Not a striking beauty but a handsome woman made more resplendent on this day in her beautiful wedding gown. Only one slight imperfection remained. The harelip which she had been born with had been operated on when she was younger and there remained only a slight hint of it. Peter Cooper had once called her "an excellent girl of humble disposition." Her serene and shy persona attested to Cooper's assessment of his granddaughter.

Amy's exquisite bridal gown was fashioned in heavy white satin brocade in moiré stripes with flowers that fell to the floor in a full round train. The front was draped in point lace and pearls and the pointed bodice was cut square at the neck filled in with lace. A gift of the bride's sisters, an exquisite diamond star with five rays shone resplendent. The long veil of dotted tulle was edged with rare and costly point lace and held by natural orange blossoms and diamond pins. Sweet and demure in character she carried a bouquet of jasmine and narcissus with a broad white satin ribbon. Her other jewels a diamond necklace, a gift from her parents and diamonds and pearls from the groom lent sparkle to the ensemble.

The bridal party passed to the large bay window, where the bride and groom stood before a floral bough where Reverend Dr. Thomas M. Peters of St. Michael's Church in Ringwood, stood to make the happy couple man and wife. Reverend Peters was an old friend of the family and had baptized the bride when a child. After the ceremony Mr. and Mrs. Green received the congratulations of their friends and relatives.

To commemorate the day, on the center table of the library lay an artistically illuminated marriage certificate, which read as follows:

This Is to Certify That
On the 15th Day of November
In the Year of Our Lord
One Thousand Eight Hundred and Eighty Six
James Olive Green of Kentucky
And
Amy Bowman Hewitt of Ringwood, New Jersey
Were United in Holy Matrimony.

Among the long list of those who affixed their names to the marriage register were Mr. Lloyd Bryce, the husband of Edith Cooper; Elizabeth Marbury, Sarah Hewitt's friend; Norvin Green, the father of the bridegroom; Mr. K.G. Lorillard from Tuxedo Park; Miss Ethel Potter; and Eleanor Mortimer.

The weather on the wedding day was so splendid that an elaborate luncheon, catered by Pinard for the myriad guests, was spread out and served to the guests seated at small tables on the porches and lawns. After the delicious meal, many guests enjoyed a leisurely walk to Mr. Hewitt's model farm and hennery. Serenaded by the popular Landers orchestra, some of the guests gaily chimed in when the band played a selection from *The Mikado* and began to hum along. It seems that a good time was had by all.

After the wedding guests had all departed, the festivities continued with the Ringwood employees, who eagerly accepted Mr. Hewitt's invitation to come up to the house. The *New York Times* on November 16, 1886, concluded, "The pretty bride, standing at one end of a large room, shook hands with everyone of them and, as they beamed with the pleasure of being in such company, they could be heard to say, 'Bless you, Miss Amy.' The bridesmaid's broke off roses and made little bouquets, which they gave to the 200 or 300 workmen, who with their families passed into another room, where each received a tasteful box of wedding cake." As tradition prescribed, the bride and groom were driven away amid a shower of rice and flowers.

A ROYAL ENTERTAINMENT

During Abram Hewitt's political career, the dining room was also the center of high society activity at Ringwood Manor. So many dignitaries were entertained there that the manor came to be called the "Little White

House." None of these social affairs was more celebrated than a big house party and dinner for the Duke and Duchess of Marlborough.

Edward recalled, "My father, when he was Mayor of New York, in 1888, had married the eighth Duke of Marlborough and the former Mrs. Lilian Warren Hamersley at City Hall. Hewitt performed the civil ceremony and due to his short stature he had to stand on tiptoe to accept the only fee he asked, which was a wedding kiss."

A friendship began from that day between the Duke and Hewitt, and the subsequent dinner at Ringwood for the royal couple was their first visit to America since the Duchess's fortune had rebuilt Blenheim. There were twenty at dinner, and the elegantly dressed women did not disappoint, but the focus of attention was on the beautiful Duchess of Marlborough. It was a sumptuous affair, with thirteen courses, appropriate silver cutlery and crystal glasses sparkling everywhere and a different wine served at each course. In those days, after dinner, it was the custom for the gentlemen to conduct the ladies to the drawing room, and then return to the dining room for smoking and liquors. On this historic occasion, Mr. and Mrs. Hewitt, the delighted hosts, outdid their hospitality.

HEWITT AND MORGAN

Throughout Abram's life, he was known for his strong moral integrity, and this example was played out time and again in business and politics. When Abram retired from the steel business to take a more active part in public life, he felt that this phase of his life was over. Edward Ringwood remembered:

> *Mr. Morgan, however, did not feel that my father was through and when the list of directors of the U.S. Steel Corporation, appeared in the newspapers, my father found that without his permission he had been named as a director. I accompanied him to Morgan's office at once, as my father had no intention of being a director.*
>
> *Mr. Morgan came to him from behind his big desk, put his arm about his shoulder and said, "Mr. Hewitt, I know why you have come to see me. You don't want to be a steel director. But you must do this for me, even if it is only for a short time. I have no honest man on the board who knows the steel business. And I must have at least one." My father replied that, if it were put that way,*

he supposed he would have to serve, but on only one condition—that he should act as he thought right and take orders from no one. Mr. Morgan agreed to this.

You would have thought that this was the end of this episode, but after a year had passed, it came time for the annual report to stockholders:

By that time, the shares of the U.S. Steel Corporation, had gone down greatly in price, and the outlook for the company was none too good. My father again went to see Morgan at his house on Madison Avenue and asked what kind of a report he intended to make. Morgan frankly told him—a whitewashing report, which would not disclose the exact status of the affairs of the company. My father then said that he must hand in his resignation, as he could not be a director of any company which did not make a full and honest report to the public on the use of the public's money, for which the directors were really trustees.

Morgan stormed up and down in his library and replied that he would like to make a complete report, but, if he did, the shock to the market would be such that he could not support the shares, and even the firm of J.P. Morgan and Company might be seriously involved. My father refused to be shaken from his ground. Finally, he announced that, when he handed in his resignation, he intended to make a statement to the press of his reasons for doing so—a statement to the effect that the directors, under the instructions of Mr. Morgan, had refused to make a full and accurate statement of the affairs of the company. Then, said my father, we'll see what will happen.

In a few days, the final director's meeting was to take place before the report would be made public:

The day before the meeting my father was very nervous. He slept not at all that night. The next morning I went down with him to his office and at ten-thirty a messenger brought a letter from Mr. Steele, Mr. Morgan's partner, saying, "I have just received the following telegram from Mr. Morgan: 'Do exactly as Mr. Hewitt directs in today's steel meeting.' Signed, J.P. Morgan." I have never seen such a weight lifted from anyone as from my father at that moment. He felt that he had won the battle for honest accounting of other people's money.

Incidentally, the firm of J.P. Morgan weathered the financial crisis. Several years later, when Mr. Hewitt was giving a big fundraising dinner at his house for the Metropolitan Museum of Art with twenty-four of New York's most distinguished men in attendance, Mr. Morgan came over to him, put his arm around his shoulders and said, "I want all these gentlemen to know that you have been my best friend. Without your advice and insistence on making complete accounts of the Steel Corporation public, I do not believe the firm J.P. Morgan and Company would be in existence today. You have saved my business career and my reputation and I want all these gentlemen to know this."

HEWITT'S RETIREMENT

In his most productive years, Hewitt's record of achievements ranked him among the great men who succeeded in establishing New York City as the epicenter of banking, politics and philanthropy. He was a leader of those who contended for reform in municipal governments, was most conspicuous for his public spirit and exerted a great influence for the good not only in New York City but also in the state. In Congress, he was a consistent defender of sound money and civil service reform; in municipal politics, he was in favor of business administrations and opposed to partisan nominations. In his administration as mayor of New York, he was a pillar of righteousness in a political world demanding compromise and pragmatism. Although his rigid devotion to his principles damaged his political fortunes, Hewitt's municipal reforms contributed to the greater good in the development of New York City.

During his long life, Abram had been the presiding genius of The Cooper Union and was its president, as well as secretary of the board of trustees. He was also a trustee of Columbia University. Accolades poured in, and he was elected president of the Columbia College Alumni Association. In 1887, his alma mater conferred on him the degree of Doctor of Laws.

After his retirement, Hewitt never quite left the public scene and devoted his energies elsewhere. He was a chairman of the board of trustees of Barnard College and a member of the executive committee of the Carnegie Institution. Andrew Carnegie himself claimed that the former mayor was "America's foremost private citizen."

In 1876 and again in 1890, Hewitt served as president of the American Institute of Mining Engineers. His friends were many, and once, in a letter from President Roosevelt, he was told, "His presence had been an inspiration and the decent performance of his duties was a heritage of honor for the city." A man of his times, Abram Stevens Hewitt was one of the most noteworthy and productive North Rockland natives in history.

Long before he died, Hewitt said, "I hope when the time comes it will be said of me that I was a statesman. Of my papers and endeavors, and of my work and speeches in Congress, I hope to be judged, and that it might be said that as a statesman I laboured. You will find when you reach my age that if you have lived up to your best judgment that is about all that a man can hope to do."

After an illness of ten days, Abram Stevens Hewitt died on January 18, 1903, at the age of eighty-one in his family residence on Lexington Avenue. He was surrounded at his bedside by his wife and children. There was a constant stream of callers at the family's residence and at the houses of Peter Cooper Hewitt at 11 Lexington Avenue and Mrs. James Olive Green at 15 Lexington Avenue. Condolences poured in, and Bishop Potter, who officiated at Hewitt's funeral, said in a tribute, "No young man had fewer privileges than Abram Stevens Hewitt, no one more nobly used his opportunities. With his large vision, wise foresight, and courage of initiative, no task was too great for him to take up." The legacy of America's foremost private citizen in the Cooper-Hewitt dynasty of New York remains a source of solid inspiration for generations to come.

PART III
The Hewitt Sisters

The Cooper Union Museum for the Arts of Decoration

The Cooper-Hewitt dynasty in New York brings us full circle to the three Hewitt sisters: Sarah Cooper Hewitt, Eleanor Garnier and Amy Hewitt Green, founders of The Cooper Union Museum for the Arts of Decoration, which was founded in 1897 on the fourth floor of The Cooper Union, Peter Cooper's free institute.

The metamorphosis of the fledgling museum into a museum of national stature is a riveting story of survival. However, the current state of the museum is of paramount interest. While the energetic and inspired sisters used their creativity and their wealth and social resources to turn their private collection into a public one, as time progressed and collections overwhelmed, The Cooper Union could no longer accommodate their museum. The Cooper Union Museum's collections eventually outgrew its space and began to conflict with the art school in regards to programming. Eventually, other departments of The Cooper Union were making financial demands, and The Cooper Union announced that it would close the museum. This led to the museum being closed on July 3, 1963. You can imagine the public outcry against the closing. Henry Francis DuPont stepped into the fray and formed the Committee to Save The Cooper Union Museum, and the American Association of Museums developed a case study about its future.

Urgencies to save the museum led to negations between Cooper Union and the Smithsonian Institution, and on October 9, 1967, Smithsonian secretary S. Dillon Ripley and Daniel Maggin, the chair of the board of trustees, signed an agreement turning over the collection and the library of the museum to the Smithsonian. The New York Supreme Court approved the agreement, and the museum officially fell under the ownership of the Smithsonian, and on July 1, 1968, it was renamed the Cooper-Hewitt Museum of Design. The name of the museum was to have yet another change, though. The following year, it was renamed the Cooper-Hewitt Museum of Decorative Arts and Design.

It seems a fitting ending to this part of the story that the Cooper-Hewitt Museum found a new home in Andrew Carnegie's commodious and stately Georgian-style mansion at Fifth Avenue and Ninetieth Street in New York City, moving there in 1970. It is sufficient to remind you that the Hewitt sisters' father, Abram Stevens Hewitt, served on the board of the Carnegie Institution, and when he died, Andrew Carnegie himself claimed that the former mayor was "America's foremost private citizen." The new location of the museum was a milestone in museum history, as it was the first Smithsonian museum outside of Washington, D.C.

Seventy-nine years after its inauguration in 1897, the first public opening of the Cooper-Hewitt Museum took place on October 7, 1976, with the exhibition Man transFORMS. Another major change was yet to come in 1994 when the museum's name was changed for the final time to the Smithsonian, Cooper-Hewitt National Design Museum. The museum is currently closed for renovations and is scheduled to reopen in 2014. During the renovation, off-site exhibitions were staged at the United Nations building and on Governors Island in New York City. Cooper-Hewitt continues its tradition as a working museum with the addition of off-site facilities such as the Cooper-Hewitt Design Center, an education facility that opened in Harlem, New York, in 2012 to bring design programming to an underserved community.

SOME HISTORICAL ACCOUNT: THE COOPER HEWITT MUSEUM FOR THE ARTS OF DECORATION

In Peter Cooper's day, New York offered little in the way of artistic and cultural enlightenment, and it was always his vision to enrich the experience of The Cooper Union students by including a museum in his school. Looking for inspiration, he was a regular visitor at curiosity museums, where he studied the wax works, historical relics, dwarfs, giants, animals and exotica. He went so far as have the stair landing at Cooper Union painted with a cyclorama of historical events, just like the one he had seen at Schudder's Museum located on Broadway at Ann Street. Venturing further, he visited "Barnum's American Museum," the emporium of P.T. Barnum, the quintessential showman, but this, too, was a thrill-seekers venue for the star attractions: the famous midgets General Tom Thumb and his bride, Lavinia Warren Bumpus.

Peter Cooper had a far greater educational purpose for his museum, but it was derailed from the onset. The museum did not at first fully materialize because the financial needs of Cooper Union itself took precedence. Sadly, Peter Cooper died in 1883 before he was able to realize his museum plan, and by necessity the project was laid aside for lack of funds, but it was never definitely abandoned. In the meantime, the Hewitt sisters' ambition matured, and they became determined to fulfill their grandfather's museum plan. Recalling their youthful aspiration, Eleanor wrote, "We were quite ignorant of the immensity of the task which we so calmly undertook. We asked for a room in which to install a Museum for the Arts of Decoration similar to the Musee des Arts Decoratif, newly opened in Paris, for the use of Cooper Union Art Class courses of instruction."

A TALE OF THREE SISTERS

The Hewitt sisters' interest in the decorative arts began at an early age. Amy, Sarah and Eleanor were spirited young women who were brought up in the Victorian era in a world of privilege and opportunity. Although they came from one of old New York's prominent families and could have easily remained society belles, their lifework led them on quite another path, one so few women of their time could have dreamed of.

The sisters did, however, have at their disposal large financial and social connections stemming from an impressive family tree. They had the benefit of their family's heritage and the influence of two important men in their lives: the patriarchs of the Cooper-Hewitt dynasty, Peter Cooper and Abram Stevens Hewitt.

The sisters evidently adored their grandfather, and when he retired, he would indulge his warm affection for them and strongly plant visions of his ambition for a museum in their fertile imaginations. No doubt the museum plan was often the subject of discussion on many occasions in the Cooper-Hewitt home, and through this intimate process, the sisters embarked as collectors at an early age.

No less influential was their father, Abram Stevens Hewitt, who like Cooper was a self-made industrialist, master iron monger, political leader and philanthropist. He is best known for his work with Cooper Union and its administration but was also a loyal supporter of the museum project.

The curious hand of fate entwining these two families formed an unusual intellectual alliance from the start as they all lived together in two residences: the Cooper mansion in New York and Ringwood Manor, their country estate. In such an arrangement, the Hewitt sisters had windows of opportunity to observe and emulate the best characteristics in the Cooper-Hewitt dynasty, from cultural pursuits to the awareness of their family's philanthropy.

The sisters' love of beautiful and exquisite workmanship came as an inheritance from those two practical and artistic men in their lives, Peter and Abram. Amy, Sarah and Eleanor were strongly influenced by their grandfather and father, and they understood the growing importance of materials and technology in an increasingly industrial age.

Abram Hewitt's French Huguenot ancestry gave the sisters an innate love of art and fine decoration, and early on he provided his daughters with exposure to exhibitions and auctions to awaken and cultivate their young minds. In the speech "The Making of a Modern Museum," given by Eleanor Garnier Hewitt at a meeting of the Wednesday Afternoon Club in 1919, she reflected on their father's nurturing: "While Cooper Union was trying to fulfill the colossal education demands of the public, two little girls with pigtails tightly braided, whose old-fashioned dresses had been cut and sewn by their mother on the first Wheeler & Wilson sewing machine, were taken regularly by their father to all places where objects of art were exhibited before their sale at auction."

Although the sisters did not attend a formal college, their education was augmented by private tutoring at home and in Europe during the family's frequent trips abroad. The Hewitts were strong Francophiles, and the sisters were taught two hours of French each day; to their advantage, they spoke flawless French.

Their curious minds were further developed in their father's personal library, which they were permitted the run of as a special privilege. Their own education in the decorative arts, Eleanor wrote, came from early and continual exposure to dozens of volumes to be found there. The precocious young girls pored through historical books, years of the *Illustrated London News* and publications such as *The Grammar of Ornamentation*, published in 1856, the defining work in decorative arts by Owen Jones, the Welsh architect and interior designer. Their appreciation for the decorative arts was further abetted by the colorful illuminations in *A Winter's Tale* and *Joseph and His Brethren*, which were among the works that aroused their interest in design.

Their father, a natural raconteur, having visited both the London Crystal Palace Exhibition of 1851 and the great Paris Exposition of 1855, would bring to life the woodcuts with storyteller descriptions to charm the sisters. Their exposure to these publications and books formed a suitable background for all later study of art and ornamentation, especially when supplemented by the *Illustrated Encyclopedia*, which filled their minds with the costumes, manners and customs of olden times in foreign countries. The wealth of their father's library also included works of great authors, including Charles Kingsley, Benjamin Disraeli and Jane Austen. At any rate, the sisters were exposed to the best of literature and artistic expression, which left an indelible impression on their young minds.

TEENAGERS AS COLLECTORS

The Hewitt sisters' interest in art and design surfaced at an early age. Unlike other young girls, who might have spent their pocket money on trinkets and amusements, Sarah and Eleanor, when merely teenagers, developed an uncanny interest in precious materials and purchased half of the Jervis Collection of textiles, ranging in date from the twelfth to the sixteenth century. They had an intuition that, as they could not afford the entire collection, the earlier portion of the textile collection would possess greater technical and artistic value than the seventeenth- and eighteenth-century part. At this time, creating a museum was far from their thoughts. For one thing, they had never seen one, yet unwittingly this purchase was an initial step in that direction, albeit they had no formal training for a museum project. Years later, Eleanor related, "It seemed easy of accomplishment, when willingness, the power of work and spending their own pocket money, appeared to be all that was required."

Although the sisters naïvely believed that they could do this by their own efforts, they stirred up interest within Peter Cooper and Abram Hewitt's circle of eminent New Yorkers and influential friends, and contacts and resources came to them quite unexpectedly. When they were old enough to travel to Europe, they were able to add to their enlightenment on the subject of the decorative arts by talking with dealers in London and Paris and with collectors such as Messieurs Bonnaffe, Alma-Tadema and Sir Frederick Leighton. They were impressed with the South Kensington Museum in London, England (now the Victoria & Albert), and its formula would later serve to set the foundation for the modest Cooper Union Museum.

The greatest inspiration for the sisters' museum was the opening of the Musee des Arts Decoratifs in the Palais de L'Industrie, newly opened in 1880 in Paris in the historic Place des Vosges. It brought about talks with the founders and Monsieur Alfred de Champeaux, the curator of the Decorative Arts Library. The directors, perhaps secretly amused at the youth and inexperience of the sisters, were nonetheless generous with their advice and time. Despite firsthand accounts of the difficulties in making the Paris museum of service to the public, it only served to arouse the sisters' strong desire to place a similar facility within the reach of American students and artisans.

When the sisters applied for a space for their museum, there was at first some reluctance to acquiesce to their request. However, The Cooper Union trustees, recalling the fact that Peter Cooper had designated one floor in his original plan for a museum, assented in the end. The sisters decided to make it a museum for the decorative arts because New York already had a natural history museum, an art museum and a historical society. The Cooper Union Museum was to have a more open-door policy for its patrons and would be free and open three days a week.

THE STATE OF DECORATIVE DESIGN

The Cooper Union Museum for the Arts of Decoration would fulfill a cultural need then lacking in New York. At that time, it was the belief by those who concerned themselves with the state of taste in America that it had fallen into a pit of ostentation and vulgarity. One needs only to recall that it was the age of Victorian clutter, overstuffed furnishings, fringed and tasseled everything, lambrequins and stuffy window decorations. The ladies and gentlemen who flaunted "taste" over vulgarity cited the Great Exhibition of the Works of Industry of All Nations in 1851 as one of the venues that was culpable for the prevalence of such vulgarity.

New York City had its own Crystal Palace of 1853, built on the present site of Bryant Park, and great crowds turned out to view the imposing building and see the thousands of exhibits of all kinds of manufactured goods from Europe and the Western Hemisphere. American taste was changed by these displays, but in the judgment of the Hewitt sisters and their like-minded contemporaries, it introduced the fussy Queen Anne style; refinement of the decorative arts was yet to come.

On the threshold of refinement of the decorative arts, the Hewitt sisters were ahead of their time and instinctively promoted their French taste in acquiring the rare and wonderful collections for their museum. However, the scheme for their museum was more than merely an adjunct of the art school at the Union; it was a way to make available to mature designers, as well as students, an opportunity to study the best examples of the decorative arts and design that they could bring together. It seems to have been the sisters' convinced opinion that American examples offered no inspiration to designers and that France, rather than England, should be the focus of their attention. As a matter of fact, they seem to have preferred to wipe the nineteenth-century slate clean and get back to the pre-industrial designs and patterns of the eighteenth century and before.

ENDORSING THE MUSEUM

The sisters also stirred up interest about their museum, and supporters emerged to endorse the museum's purpose. Eleanor recalled, "One of their friends, Elizabeth Bisland in 1896 wrote a pamphlet called 'Plan of the Proposed Cooper Union Museum,' which was presented to The Cooper Union trustees at their annual meeting. She made it clear that in her judgment, as did the Hewitt sisters believe, that the state of decorative arts in American was appalling and that salvation was to be found in emulating the French, and most specifically the example of the Musee des Arts Decoratifs in Paris." Miss Bisland attested further that "not only were American designers ill-educated in their art, but the 'public standard of taste' was in dire need to be pulled up by its shabby bootstraps to a level that Miss Bisland believed prevailed in Europe." In fact, she wrote, "For the best work in decoration we still need to depend on foreign skill and taste."

The sisters' believed, as Eleanor wrote, that "America was entering a new era, and that Cooper Union's Museum for the Arts of Decoration was the pioneer blazing the trail."

THE MUSEUM FOR THE ARTS OF DECORATION

The fledgling museum, opened informally in 1895 with little fanfare, was given its official launching in 1897 as The Cooper Union Museum for the Arts of Decoration. Though the sisters' wealth came from industrialization, the museum's focus was the rebirth of old styles from a world created by artisans and craftsmen.

Although at first the museum was a mere gallery on the fourth floor in The Cooper Union, in time the entire fourth floor was given over to the museum collections that the sisters had been actively amassing during their travels. They were excellent researchers and studied the collections wherever the decorative arts were displayed, be it museum, gallery or private holdings. In so doing, they acquired a connoisseur's taste, and influenced by their French sensibilities, they evaluated objects for their beauty, exceptional quality and workmanship. From the start, textiles were their foremost interest, but they additionally chose the best-designed wallpapers, porcelains, architectural and decorative drawings, laces, furniture, glass, pottery, musical instruments, furniture and even bird cages, all of which formed the original collection for their museum. The sisters' intuitive gift for collecting made it possible for them to acquire a huge assortment of decorative objects, which was aided by the fact that in the late 1800s few American museums were interested in acquiring decorative arts. Therefore, the sisters had found a unique niche and little competition in purchasing rare decorative works of art for their museum.

Eleanor recalled, "Then came a wonderful series of happenings. Manufacturers and dealers came forward with unsolicited help and many prominent firms gave objects suitable to make small exhibits covering various branches of textiles and the ornamental trades."

Since its inception, the museum was to make all objects, books and information available to students, scholars and collectors of all kinds. The Museum for the Arts of Decoration was kept open at night, particularly to accommodate workers who were employed by day— the first museum to do so. "There were to be," Eleanor said, "no tedious restrictions and formalities to be gone through; anyone who stopped at the General Office of The Cooper Union and asked for a card was welcome."

STEWARDS OF THE MUSEUM

Although Sarah Cooper and Eleanor Garnier Hewitt became the principal founders of the museum, there were other Hewitt women who became early stewards of the museum's development. With the help and encouragement of their mother, Sarah Amelia Hewitt, and their older sister, Amy Hewitt Green, the enterprise took full realization.

The Hewitt family was not exempt from making contributions to the museum, and the first of many gifts came from their father and mother. Eleanor particularly remembered her mother's contribution: "Mrs. Hewitt suffered the most, and as she looked around at her devastated house, would often say, 'I wonder where that is?' pointing to an empty space or, when visiting the museum exclaim, 'Didn't I once have something like that?' thinking she recognized some cherished object." Throughout her life, Mrs. Hewitt continued to part with her treasures, and when the museum opened, she donated a fine lace collection.

After Amy married Dr. James Olive Green in 1886 in a great society wedding at Ringwood, she temporarily left the Cooper-Hewitt circle and relinquished active participation in the museum's progress but not her lifelong interest and contribution. With the exception of seven winters spent in Europe with her husband, after her marriage she devoted much of her time to the work of the Ladies' Advisory Council of the Woman's Art School and the School of Typewriting and Stenography of The Cooper Union, of which she was secretary. She had also aroused in her two younger sisters their profound interest in The Cooper Union and desire to be of service to it, and her influence bolstered Sarah's and Eleanor's ambition to fulfill their grandfather's museum plan.

Thereafter, Eleanor and Sarah remained on a steady course and were most involved with the development of the museum and the acquisition of its treasures. They understood the growing importance of materials and technology, and their mission in life was focused on fulfilling their grandfather Peter Cooper's vision and to complete the work he originally planned. The sisters always said that "they were prompted to found the Museum as a tribute to their grandfather, who had wanted 'Galleries of Art' in Cooper Union."

DONORS BEARING GIFTS

Then came a wonderful series of happenings. As the new museum's reputation gained recognition, other donors came forward with unsolicited help, as did many other public-spirited individuals who sent gifts and sums of money large and small, all of which contributed to the growth of the fledgling museum.

Such was the sisters' enthusiasm that individuals on both sides of the Atlantic fell in line bearing gifts, including the great Parisian couturier Worth, which contributed textiles. Soon after the museum was opened, Mr. George A. Hearn, the founder of Hearn's Department Store, which stood for years on Fourteenth Street in old New York, came to see what this new museum was all about. Later, when the Hewitt sisters visited his office, they were quite startled and at the same time pleased by a remark he made. "You have undertaken far more than you know," he said to Miss Eleanor and Miss Sarah, "but I am going to help you." He was better than his word through the remainder of his life, both with gifts of suitable objects and with generous donations of money each year. These large sums, given so freely by Mr. Hearn at a time when such extraordinary decorative objects were still procurable, made it possible for the museum to attract sufficient interest and also bring in unpaid intellectual help to document the collections. These volunteers, the educated minds of some of society's belles and like-minded friends, sequenced objects, wrote labels and provided services likened to that of a paid high-class assistant who worked with the Hewitt sisters in categorizing the collections.

Eleanor and Sarah were hands-on curators. They proceeded each morning to the museum and plunged into the dusty work of cutting and filing and pasting pictures of furniture, mantels, draperies and porcelains and laces—anything that might be useful to inspire designers and students.

A Moment in History

Coincidentally, at the time of the opening of the Hewitt sisters' museum, there was a movement to teach women about the arts of decoration and to engage them professionally in it as an acceptable profession. Other inspired women came into prominence at that time to support the trend. Candace Wheeler, who was one of America's first female interior and textile designers, like the Hewitt sisters helped to open up the field of interior design. While the Cooper Hewitt Museum for the Arts of Decoration provided a wealth of inspiration in its research collections, Wheeler founded the Society of Decorative Art and worked to promote the value of and demand for arts and crafts objects. At the same time, the American author Edith Wharton, in collaboration with the young architect Ogden Codman Jr., published her first book, *The Decoration of Houses*, and by the 1890s, magazine articles were encouraging women to pursue careers in the field.

J.P. Morgan's Largesse

Their father, Abram, being on the high social strata of society, was a member of the best clubs in New York, including the elite Metropolitan Club, the Players Club and the Century Club. It was fortuitous that he associated with people in high places in New York society because chance brought about a meeting between Mr. J. Pierpont Morgan and Mr. Hewitt at a men's dinner. The former, aware that Hewitt's daughters were engaged in acquiring artifacts for the museum, asked in his usual abrupt and impulsive way, "Mr. Hewitt, what are your daughters interested in?"

Writing about this meeting, Eleanor recalled her father's reply: "They are negotiating the purchase of the unique Badia Collection of textiles for sale in Barcelona." Hewitt's response prompted Morgan's unexpected request that all the papers relating to it should be sent to him that night, as he was sailing for Europe the next day. A man of large gestures, he understood the sisters' cause, and a few weeks later, Morgan cabled Mr. Hewitt: "Have purchased the Badia Collection in Barcelona, also the Vives Collection of Madrid, and the Stanislas Baron Collection of Paris. I do this to give your daughters pleasure." With Morgan's purchase, The Cooper Union Museum jumped to the rank of

London's South Kensington Museum in the quality of its textiles and acquired the most important collection of medieval textiles in the world, surpassing collections in museums in Lyon, France, and Berlin, Germany.

MORE GENEROUS DONORS

It seemed that many more people of consequence were eager to contribute to the museum. As if by magic, Munroe & Company of New York and Paris, one of the oldest-established banking houses and a most public-spirited firm, voluntarily came forth to handle the correspondence and negotiations for an extraordinary Italian collection. Signor Piancastelli, curator of the Borghese Gallery in Rome, had decided to dispose of his collection consisting of four thousand drawings of the seventeenth and eighteenth centuries, including the sketchbooks by Italian artists and hundreds of original designs for schemes of decoration for every branch of the ornamental arts. The purchase price of $4,000 was contributed by "friends of the museum," while all the details of the transaction, packing and shipping were facilitated by Monroe & Company to bring this collection to America.

It is too often believed that money is all that is needed to bring together an art collection. Not so with the Hewitt sisters. Had they not had the qualities of knowledge, love and persistence, they would not have obtained the extraordinary Leon Decloux Collection of ornament drawings, which the Parisian saved for the museum.

When the sisters were in Europe for one of their annual studying/ buying trips on behalf of their museum, they attended a luncheon in Paris, where they were introduced to Jean Leon Decloux, an architect and decorative arts collector whose taste and judgment were considered supreme in Paris. He was impressed with the idea that The Cooper Union Museum was not conceived for the sole delight of the curator but rather had a far-reaching purpose in its use by the general public. Finding the attempt by the two young women to create a museum quite interesting, he invited them to his villa at Serves to see his boiseries, porcelains, ironwork, glass, wonderful furniture and bibelots of all kinds.

As Eleanor remembered, his gesture was meant "just to give them pleasure." However, this was just an exploratory visit, as he had no idea of disposing of his collections, but he gladly accepted the small sums the sisters could send, to give them all the advantage of his taste and knowledge in the selection of items for the museum. This advisory relationship grew into a business pact, and within a year, Decloux had an ongoing relationship with the Hewitt sisters, functioning as their Paris agent for the purchase of decorative arts materials for the museum's collection. The objects that he procured in 1911 and 1921 for such moderate amounts soon placed the museum in the first rank and formed the foundation of the Cooper-Hewitt's Rococo and Neoclassical collections of works on paper. Later, Decloux ceded to the museum many of his own priceless treasures, including ornament prints by such important Rococo designers as Meisonnier, Jacques de Lajoue, Alexis Peyrotte, Jean-François Cuvillies and Johann Michael Hoppenhaupt II. Today, Cooper-Hewitt's Rococo holdings rank among the best in the United States.

So sensational was the acquisition of the collection that Eleanor wrote from Ringwood Manor to Mr. Morgan, who had so generously acquired the Badia Collection for the museum, "My dear Mr. Morgan: I enclose a cutting about the Decloux collection which was presented to the Cooper Union Museum by the Council. In the autumn we shall hope to have the pleasure of showing it to you in place. With best wishes for a delightful summer. Always Sincerely, Eleanor G. Hewitt, July 5, 1912."

THE AMERICAN MASTERS

In building the collection as an educational resource for artists and designers, the Hewitt sisters were particularly interested in works that reveal the creative process. Their interest in collecting, therefore, extended beyond the arts of decoration to include the works of American artists. At a time when few collectors were giving attention to the drawings of American masters, they acquired more than two thousand oil and pencil sketches by Frederick E. Church, donated by Church's son, Louis P. Church, with the result that the museum has the largest collection of American nineteenth-century drawings in the country. When Winslow Homer died, his brother, Charles Savage Homer, gave to the museum all that remained in the artist's studio—more than three hundred paintings, watercolors and drawings. In this manner, the museum came to own the largest collection of the artist's work. They included every aspect of Homer's work from the days before the Civil War (during which he was an artist-reporter for *Harper's Weekly*) to the close of his career in 1909. The museum was also presented with nearly one hundred drawings and watercolors by the landscapist Thomas Moran, whose love of the spacious West and his depiction of it caused a Wyoming mountain to be named in his honor.

SOCIETY LADIES CONTRIBUTE

Word about the museum was spreading among elite circles, and a new batch of contributors arrived on the scene. Interest in the museum grew steadily among the society ladies of old New York, who wished to help with financial contributions. Of particular note, a genteel lady provided payment at the customhouse for a collection of rare French porcelains and faiences. When questioned about her payment, she said, "Oh, I always like old porcelains best." One day, another charming New Yorker, Miss Eleanor Blodgett, asked to be shown the museum and spent a delightful morning with the directors. Upon leaving the museum, she hesitated and, with a coquettish flair, drew from her muff an envelope and at the same instant announced, "I wish to make a Memorial for my Mother." She said that her mother, Mrs. William Tilden Blodgett, one of the most public-spirited women of her day, would have considered it a privilege and a high honor to have her name connected to The Cooper Union. The check was for $10,000, and this large sum of money made the purchase of the Leon Decloux Collection of drawings an absolute certainty.

Financial backing for the purchase of decorative arts poured in from many other benevolent sources. Each time the Hewitt sisters went to Europe, the generous Mr. Jacob H. Schiff and Mr. Thomas Snell sent large checks to buy the best that could be found in the way of fine things to enhance the beauty and working qualities of the young museum's holdings. The purchase of art books facilitated by the generous donation of Mrs. Robert Stuart enriched the museum's reference library, adding to its priceless collection of ancient and modern illustrated books for study. Pads and pencils were on the tables for making notes and sketches. Help also came in unsolicited fashion—since many of the books on the decorative arts were in foreign languages, a number of volunteers generously undertook to translate them "to help along the work of the museum."

A Practical Laboratory

They called their museum "a practical working laboratory." The Hewitt sisters' interest was divided between collecting and having what they collected available for accessible use by those to whom the objects might mean the most. The sisters put "use" first and the prestige of their collections second. In those days, when directors of American museums were more concerned with establishing palaces of art, the Hewitt sisters were ahead of their time. Just five years after the museum opened, Miss Sally reported to The Cooper Union trustees: "While the number of visitors and workers at the Museum has not increased this season, it is gratifying to find that the people for whose use it was created have worked there more than last year, thus proving that it meets their requirements." She found that the "workers," as she called them to distinguish them from the students of the Union, showed more intelligence than previously in selecting better models to copy or a suggestion for design.

The Mineral Collection and Laboratory, Cooper Union for the Advancement of Science & Art. *Courtesy of the Library of Congress, Historic American Buildings Survey.*

This illustration shows Puck standing next to a statue of Peter Cooper in front of The Cooper Union building; Puck is holding a paper that states, "Puck suggests a few outlets for overflowing incomes." Crowds of working-class men and women and disadvantaged youths in need of proper education fill the sides, while in the center throngs of people stream toward the entrances to The Cooper Union building. *Courtesy of the Library of Congress.*

Everything was done to encourage the use of the museum to make materials available and the room pleasant to work in. "The collections are displayed in the simplest way for study and comparison," Miss Sarah reported. She and her colleagues arranged the objects chronologically by styles of ornament so that even if the student did not read the labels, their progression would be evident. For instance, Sarah wrote, "Furniture Mounts: In each period designs with horns of plenty, no matter how obscure, placed together, show one type of design; fantastic animals, another; musical instruments, allegorical motifs, garlands and wreaths, foliage scrolls, rosettes, demonstrate the variety of treatment possible in one simple motive."

The Hewitt Sisters

Museum for Use

The museum's coffers were burgeoning with treasures, but the entire concept of the "museum for use" was paramount to serve students, artists, craftsman, scholars and collectors of all kinds. Restrictions were eliminated, except in cases where it was necessary to protect certain objects. The museum, kept open at night for workers and students, was the first museum to do so, and a special plea was made by Eleanor to the trustees that workers be given a card for direct access to the museum rather than signing in on the ground floor. The literary aids of hundreds of reference and scrapbooks and of art periodicals placed on tables with no hampering restrictions as to their use put every resource at the service of the public. "Every hour and minute that the Museum is open, are working hours and minutes" was Eleanor's observation.

Russell Lynes, managing editor of *Harper's Magazine*, wrote:

By 1910 the "Encyclopedic Scrap Books" already numbered more than 1,000 volumes containing millions of reproductions of designs, supplemented in later years by hundreds of thousands of slides and photographs. (Should you, for example, like to see how the hummingbird or calla lily has been adapted for use by designers; the museum can speedily produce hundreds of examples for you.) As these extraordinary archives grew so did the collection of drawings to more than 30,000, and prints to more than 20,000. So also grew the collections of textiles and decorative and useful objects, of games and birdcages, of furniture and frivolities and vanities. There is a remarkable 17th-century lunette of wrought iron and elaborate Victorian parlour furniture of laminated wood and veneer by American designer, J.H. Belter.

While the Hewitt sisters were ambitious for their museum, they were not stuffy and added a degree of whimsicality to their collection. They liked games and illusions and toys, the more ingeniously designed to surprise and titillate the eye the better, and so there are peepshows, magic lanterns, puppets and kaleidoscopes and Zoetrope's, little drawings that if flicked make moving pictures.

New points of view brought new arrangements and exhibits, enabling the Museum for the Arts of Decoration to attract many other generous donors, including Peter Cooper's granddaughter (Lloyd Bryce's wife), Edith Cooper Bryce, who donated art and objects from the Palace of Fontainebleau.

The beautiful art gallery and drawing room at The Cooper Union for the Advancement of Science & Art. *Courtesy of the Library of Congress, Historic American Buildings Survey.*

Eleanor fondly reflected on the museum's mission: "Peter Cooper placed upon the seal of Cooper Union with the professional pride of a Master Workman, this simple and touching device, 'Founded by a Mechanic of New York,' and his granddaughters hope the seal of the Museum may someday also bear the inscription, 'Founded by Hereditary Works in the Same Tradition.'"

A FASHIONABLE SHOP

One interesting way the museum acquired other financial support stemmed from an attempt to find ways for young women who had graduated from The Cooper Union Art School to earn a living. A spirited woman, Mrs. Montgomery Hare, whose father, John C. Parsons, was chairman of the board of Cooper Union, joined forces with the Hewitt sisters to open a shop that they called, in the fashion of the day, Au Panier Fleuri, to execute commissions from decorators who wanted panels, lampshades and other ornamental objects for their clients. The shop proved successful and made money, and prominent interior decorators, including Elsie de Wolfe, were patronizing it. By the time the shop was selling more than $45,000 worth of its products and making a profit of $7,500, a portion of it was turned back to The Cooper Union for use of the Hewitts as they saw fit for their museum. "To achieve good results," Miss Eleanor reported to the museum's council, "Cooper Union graduates employed by 'Au Panier Fleuri' also work in the museum every few weeks." Following in the tradition of retail selling, it is interesting to note here that the Smithsonian, Cooper-Hewitt National Design Museum opened an online retail shop in 2012.

THE MUSEUM COUNCIL

The spectrum of acquisitions in the museum needed to be continually expanded as its uses grew, and help seemed to flood in from unexpected sources. Eleanor reported that a most practical friend named Thomas Snell, for one, volunteered to have the walls and woodwork of the museum painted. Typical of the largesse of this man, when the job was done, he sent a complimentary receipted bill and a generous check to purchase materials for the collection.

By far the most noteworthy of these benefactors was their old friend George A. Hearn, who early on had volunteered to help them financially. The legend goes that he was an avid collector of paintings by his American contemporaries. At one point, he offered the collection to the Metropolitan Museum of Art, but the museum staff was not interested in purchasing what the Ashcan School artists were producing. That proved fortuitous for the Hewitt sisters' museum, as the collection became part of their museum's holdings.

Mr. Hearn was an influential backer, and when he organized a council for The Cooper Union Museum, the sisters were initially against the idea and fought him for nearly three years. You can imagine the sisters' distress at such a suggestion. They did not like the idea of a governing body looking over their shoulders, so to speak, and telling them what to do. "Well," Mr. Hearn said, "I don't care what you think; I will form the Council and give you money to spend."

Finally, the sisters agreed, with one important condition: that on the council, in addition to persons of influence and affluence, there should be a committee of artists "to control their recommendations for expenditure." It is sufficient to say that the respect that artists had for the museum brought forth prominent names for the judging of incoming works. Louis Comfort Tiffany, the then famous painter and decorator of interiors best known for his stained-glass lamps, was among the first to be on the council, as were sculptor Daniel Chester French, muralist Edwin H. Blashfield and portraitist John W. Alexander.

At its inception, the council did not include women, but prominent businessmen, collectors, lawyers and New York City's leaders were counted among the individuals who put emphasis on design in the collections that they acquired. Eleanor reported to the council, "They will furnish inspiration forever to seekers of authentic documentary knowledge of design and technical skill from original sources." The sisters' "committee of artists" concept may well have inspired Candace Wheeler, who similarly established the Committee on Design, the judging panel for incoming works to her Society of Decorative Art.

THE CROWNING GLORY

The *New York Times* published an enthusiastic article under the headline "Cooper Union's Crowning Glory: Its Museum of Decorative Art." The piece was timed to coordinate with The Cooper Union commencement in May 1907, and Mr. Hearn would have approved of this opportunity to publicize the museum's holdings. The *Times* said of the museum that it was "the most prosperous year in Cooper's long history of usefulness." Many New Yorkers were impressed that there was no red tape, no restrictions with which the collections might be seen. In addition, there were objects that were on loan for short periods, such as Miss Elsie de Wolfe's collection of shoes and slippers of the sixteenth, seventeenth and eighteenth centuries, as well as footwear of the Orient, which proved to be of special interest to theatrical designers and illustrators.

Miss Eleanor noted, "Two private boarding schools have sent classes to visit with their art governesses, which is taking a step towards giving a knowledge of styles to those who will probably become patronesses and employers of much artistic labor." The number that mattered most to her, however, was the number of "workers" (serious professional visitors), which had quadrupled from 80 to 350. Nothing gratified the Hewitt sisters more than the transformation of the objects in the museum into practical, commercial results by the pencils and brushes of those who used the collections, who pored over the scrapbooks and minutely examined the pieces of textiles, the casts and the drawings of architectural and decorative details. She proudly displayed objects, designs and photographs of things actually made (for the market) from originals in the museum. She also told the council members that they could not have foreseen that a late seventeenth-century Dutch decorative flower would be copied each day and that portions of it would reappear in many decorative schemes.

HISTORICAL ACQUISITIONS

In the first year of the museum's existence, it published a catalogue of a remarkable collection of prints bequeathed to it by George Campbell Cooper, Peter Cooper's nephew and business partner. It was the foundation of the museum's rare and varied collection of prints including thirty-eight Durer engravings and four woodcuts, fifty Rembrandts and dozens and dozens more items.

The Cooper Hewitt Museum for the Arts of Decoration soon became the repository for some rather extraordinary collections. Soon after the Hewitts purchased the Piancastelli drawings, Mr. Edward D. Brandegee of Boston brought more than twice as many drawings to show the sisters. Sometime later, Brandegee's wife came to the museum with two boxes she offered to sell containing 8,200 of the drawings from Piancastelli, about which the then curator wrote, "With inconspicuous omissions the entire collection has been united."

Other generous donors continued to come forth, further stocking the coffers of the museum with rare and wonderful treasures.

Before Miss Eleanor died, she made a glowing report to the council on the state of the Union's museum. "Unexpected and exciting 'miracles,'" she said, "have frequently happened during the history of the museum, yet the age of miracles continues." The legacy of The Cooper Union Museum for the Arts of Decoration is forever written in the fabric of the history of the Cooper-Hewitt dynasty.

THE LADIES

The Hewitt sisters also acquired nicknames. Family and close friends affectionately referred to Eleanor Garnier Hewitt as "Miss Nelly" and to Sarah Cooper Hewitt as "Miss Sally." Collectively, the sisters shared a unique bond, and they spent most of their time and fortune searching the world for additions to the museum's collections. They chose careers over marriage as pioneering women determined to succeed; perhaps they were the first to embark as curatrixes of a museum. The sisters' métier was art, and throughout their lifetimes, their devotion to The Cooper Union Museum for the Arts of Decoration was their paramount cause célèbre. It was not merely a diversion in the social environs of their lifestyle; it also seemed to be their destiny from the start of their childhood interest in textiles.

Eleanor Garnier Hewitt's middle name reflects her French Huguenot lineage, but in some instances, because the family's surname was Anglicized, I have found that Eleanor is also referred to as Eleanor Gurnee Hewitt. The sisters' French-English ancestry was the foundation of their creative development and inspired their love for collecting fine art and decorative treasures for their museum. No less was their appreciation for the fine art of handcraftsmanship instilled by their grandfather, John Hewitt, who descended from a long line of distinguished English cabinetmakers.

Upon taking a closer look at the Hewitt sisters' personalities, we can understand the forces that framed their character. Not only were the Hewitt girls precocious, they were, by New York standards of the day, quite eccentric. However, to understand the museum, it is important to understand the young ladies who conceived and nursed it into reality.

AMY HEWITT GREEN

Eleanor and Sarah Hewitt have rightfully been given substantial credit for assuming the responsibilities of establishing the Museum for the Arts of Decoration. However, Amy Hewitt was also involved from the start—though she had limited involvement after her marriage to James O. Green.

Amy was the eldest child of Peter Cooper's daughter, Amelia, and was born at his residence on Lexington Avenue, where she always lived in order to be as

Amy Hewitt Green. *Courtesy of The Cooper Union.*

close as possible to her parents and grandfather, who formed a close alliance with his first grandchild. In the memoriam section in the 1923 annual report of The Cooper Union, her characteristics are revealed:

As a small child, Amy endeared herself especially to her grandfather by her winning ways and unusual intelligence. As soon as she was old enough, Peter Cooper made her his constant companion, frequently driving her and himself down to the Cooper Union, in his one-horse four-wheel carriage, with its open front. This vehicle was so well known to all the old New Yorkers that it was not an uncommon sight. Amy went with him all over his beloved building, during the daily visits which he so rarely missed. Then later, although still a very young girl, she accompanied him to the Free Lectures, held every Saturday evening in the Great Hall of the Cooper Union. In spite of this severe mental training, which most high spirited children would have resented, Amy's invariable patience, sweetness of disposition, together with a generous thirst for knowledge never failed her. After she married Amy devoted much of her time to the work of the Ladies' Advisory Council of the Woman's Art School and of the School for Typewriting and Stenography of the Cooper Union. No personal or money sacrifice was too great for her. It was largely owing to her profound interest in museum that first aroused in her two younger sisters, Sarah and Eleanor, the desire to also be of service to it.

Amy was the only Hewitt daughter to wed. Her society wedding to Dr. James O. Green, the future president of Western Union Telegraph, was held at the family's Ringwood estate in 1886 and is the subject of a section in Part II of this book. Amy and James O. Green were the parents of two children, Norvin Hewitt Green and Eleanor Margaret Green. Eleanor Margaret was born in 1895, the second child of Amy, who named her daughter after her sister Eleanor Garnier Hewitt. Eleanor Margaret later married Prince Viggo of Denmark, and through this marriage, she acquired the title Princess Viggo of Denmark and became related to the late Diana, Princess of Wales, on her maternal grandmother's side.

A Royal Wedding

When Amy and James's daughter, Eleanor Margaret Green, traveled abroad one summer, she met the prince of Denmark, and a fairytale romance ensued when she was visiting her cousin, Baroness Ernst Schilling, in Copenhagen in 1923. Her meeting with the prince came about in the most natural manner: Prince Viggo fell in love with Eleanor Margaret and proposed. Following repeated press speculations and denials about their engagement, the subject of a royal wedding was at first denied by the Green family. An Associated Press story from December 27, 1923, reported:

> *It was during Miss Green's visit to Copenhagen last summer that she first met Prince Viggo. She was a guest of the United States Minister to Denmark, Dr. John Dyneley Prince and Mrs. Prince, friends of the Green family, who are her neighbors in the Ramapo Hills section. The Prince Country estate in Sterlington, N.Y., is not far away from Ringwood Manor. Like the other members of his family, Prince Viggo was a frequent guest of the American Legation. Throughout the American girl's stay the couple met often at the Legation and at sporting events. They yachted together and were seen at many race meetings.*

The Official Announcement

The following year, all speculation about the engagement was confirmed. An official announcement appeared in the newspapers bylined as Copenhagen, February 9: "It was officially announced today that King Christian and the Privy Council of Denmark had sanctioned the engagement of Christian,

Adolph, Georg HRH Prince Viggo of Denmark and Miss Eleanor Margaret Green. Miss Green is a member of a noted New York family, tracing back to Peter Cooper, remembered both as a merchant and philanthropic founder of Cooper Union."

The royal wedding of Eleanor Margaret and Prince Viggo became the headline of celebrity news. The prince was described as being "allied to all the reigning houses of Europe." His father's brothers were king of Denmark and king of Greece, respectively, and the sisters had become Queen Alexandra of Britain and empress of Russia. Prince Viggo's brother was married to Countess Mathilde de Bergolo of Italy, sister-in-law to the king of Italy's eldest daughter. Impressive as these royal family connections were, the prince, because he married a commoner, renounced his royal prerogative and his remote right of succession to the Danish throne.

Miss Green's ancestry brought to the marriage an impressive family tree that shaped the Cooper-Hewitt dynasty. The *New York Times* on June 11, 1924, reported:

> *Her ancestors have become a part of America's natural history in the realms of invention, of great commercial industry, civic duties and wide benefactions. Miss Green, the daughter of a physician, counts among her relatives a wizard of electric science, the late Peter Cooper Hewitt, her late mother's brother; also an uncle, Edward Ringwood Hewitt, deep in inventions and her aunts, the Misses Sarah and Eleanor Hewitt, who keep up The Forges founded by their grandfather, Peter Cooper, the estate inherited through their parents, the late Mr. and Mrs. Abram Stevens Hewitt. The Misses Hewitt also continues the family interest in Cooper Union, a boon to those desirous of a free education that was founded by Peter Cooper. Miss Green's forebears have also been identified since Colonial days. She is a direct descendant of the Green family of Culpepper County, Virginia, which was founded by Robert Green during the reign of Queen Anne of England.*

The festive announcement of the engagement of the couple was made in New York at a dinner given for Prince Viggo by the Misses Eleanor and Sarah Hewitt, aunts of Eleanor Margaret, at their home at 9 Lexington Avenue. Some of the dinner guests included Mr. and Mrs. J. Pierpont Morgan, Mrs. Cooper Hewitt, Mr. and Mrs. Henry White and Miss Caroline King Duer, to name a few. In the midst of the dinner, Dr. Green rose from his place to announce the engagement to the assembled company. The nuptial celebrations continued with a dinner for Prince Valdemar and the members of his family, given by Mrs. Peter Cooper Hewitt at her home at 11 Lexington Avenue.

New Yorkers eagerly awaited the royal wedding, and its celebrity status made it a spectator sensation. The marriage of Eleanor Margaret and Prince Viggo of Denmark took place on June 10, 1924, in Calvary Church, Fourth Avenue and Twenty-first Street, New York. With the marriage, Eleanor Margaret Green, the great-granddaughter of Peter Cooper and the granddaughter of Amelia and Abram Stevens Hewitt, became allied to the royal families of England, Italy, Greece and the Scandinavian countries. The Danish king announced that Prince Viggo and his future wife would bear the titles of Count and Countess of Rosenberg and that Miss Green would henceforth be addressed as Eleanor Margaret HRH Princess Viggo of Denmark.

Princess Viggo of Denmark: Spectacular Spectators

The turnout of New York society and the general surge of public spectators overwhelmed the city. The *New York Times* covered the event with this huge headline: "Prince Viggo Weds an American Girl, Notable Gathering of Society as Miss Green becomes Danish Nobleman's Bride, Great Throng at Church, Streets and Windows Crowded and Police Are Needed to Clear the Way for Guests." The paper reported, "There has probably never been recorded a marriage in the history of New York Society of such importance, and it is the first time that a person of royal birth has taken an American bride in this city."

The family rounded up thirty broughams for the occasion; it was the last wedding reception in New York for which that many guests were driven up by horses. The whole district along Lexington Avenue from Twenty-second Street to Gramercy Park and the west side of Fourth Avenue, opposite the church, was congested with people eager to see the American girl who was to become a real princess and whose husband had renounced his chances of succession to the Danish throne in order to marry her. It was an event of colossal scale, and a holiday was declared in hundreds of offices. For two hours, stenographers, bookkeepers and office messenger boys looked down on the animated scene from the skyscrapers.

In keeping with tradition, simplicity and elegance ruled the bride's wedding attire. Eleanor Margaret wore a gown with simple lines of cream-colored charmeuse, with panels down the front of old point Duchess, which had adorned her mother's wedding gown; the court train was lined with fine tucks of soft white chiffon. She also wore her mother's wedding veil of old point appliqué and a simple strand of perfectly matched pearls. In place of a bouquet, the bride carried an ivory-bound prayer book to which was attached a small cluster of orange blossoms, a traditional wedding choice representing faithfulness and innocence and a custom inaugurated by Queen Victoria when she married Prince Albert.

The newspaper columns brimmed with descriptions of the wedding. The *New York Times* noted on June 11, 1924:

> *There was a certain tradition and quaintness about the wedding which made it unique in the annals of New York Society. Peter Cooper's old landau with its coat of arms, three owls on a shield, carried Miss Green to the church and brought her home again with the prince by her side. This carriage was used by the late Colonel Theodore Roosevelt upon his inauguration, and the Hewitt family have not used it for the past fourteen years. Perched with much dignity upon the driver's seat with orange blossoms as boutonnieres, were the two retainers in the family, Michael Whalen the driver, and Michael Rollins, the footman.*
>
> *As both her parents were deceased the wedding reception was held at the old Hewitt house, 9 Lexington Avenue for 1500 guests. It was hosted by the Princess's aunts, Miss Sarah Cooper and Miss Eleanor Garnier Hewitt. The crowds of the spectators were so dense around the Hewitt mansion that they prevented the invited guests to the reception from entering the house. It was not until a mounted policeman had ridden upon the sidewalk and cleared the entrance to the house that the guests could enter.*

Young women who dreamed of marrying a prince were counted among the more than five hundred girls, students of the Manhattan Trade School for Girls, who filled the windows of the twelve-story school building directly opposite the Hewitt residence and cheered the bride and her prince. The tumult of the girls' voices could be heard for several blocks. Reserves from the Twenty-first Precinct kept the large crowd of curious in check. However, there were times upon the arrival of some important personage—like an attaché of the Danish delegation, especially in fancy dress uniform—when the women would burst through the lines, and it was all the police could do to keep back the surging mass of people.

Eleanor Margaret's aunts, Sarah and Eleanor, who had taken charge and planned the wedding, decorated the mansion with festive bouquets among the heirlooms and antiques. It was the home of the bride's grandparents, the late Abram S. Hewitt, one-time mayor of New York, and his wife, Amelia, Peter Cooper's daughter.

Elaborating on the reception, the *New York Times* further described the festivities:

> *The many guests approached the reception rooms by the wide marble staircase and were received in the blue room by the Misses Hewitt and Prince Viggo's father, Prince Valdemar, uncle of King Christian and Count of Rosenberg, and a cousin of King George of England. The diplomatic service of Denmark was represented by the charge d'Affaires of Denmark, Kal Helmer-Peterson and his wife; the Danish Consulate in New York was represented by George Bech, the Counsel General and his daughter Miss Elinor Bech plus a host of numerous dignitaries. There were many brilliant uniforms covered with decorations and costumes of the women were of the latest spring fashions. Immediate relatives of the bride's side were Erskine Hewitt, Mr. and Mrs. Edward Ringwood Hewitt and their son Ashley Hewitt; Mr. and Mrs. Charles E. Hewitt; Mrs. Charles W. Cooper; Mr. and Mrs. Schuyler Schieffelin and the Misses Mary and Barbara Schieffelin. The bride and bridegroom received the congratulations of their friends standing at the north end of the main drawing room at the west of the house where there were masses of Spring flowers, blue delphinium predominating. In the long room at the east end of the house, which sometimes is referred to as the theatre, as tradition decreed, there were displayed the many gifts received by the bride. There were great quantities of silver, fine porcelain, linens, glass, books, hunting pictures, many superb fans, engravings and paintings, but what seemed to create greater interest were the cable messages from the royal relatives in Europe.*

Eventually, the bridal pair donned their traveling attire, and the Prince and Princess Viggo left the house, passing through a double row of friends on the broad stairway. Guests pelted them with rice, and many followed them in limousines. The couple escaped to Ringwood Manor, where the master bedroom had been decorated festively with pink floral chintz for the honeymoon. Prince Viggo and his bride later sailed for England, where they visited his royal relatives, including the Dowager Queen Alexandra of England and his grandmother, the Duchesse de Chartres. They then settled down in Denmark at Bernstorff Palace, described as being surrounded by a large park of several hundred acres in the country, as both were devoted to outdoor sports. It is said that the princely newlyweds were popular in Denmark. As would be expected, the new princess, brought up on the

Cooper-Hewitt philanthropic principles, became deeply involved in charity work and was soon "Princess Peggy" to everybody.

SARAH COOPER HEWITT

The Hewitt sisters were unique for their time. They were highly individualistic and had strong personalities that did not clash but instead complemented each other. Their genre of feminism paved the way for a new breed of independent women.

Sarah Cooper Hewitt, or "Miss Sally," as she was affectionately called, was a very accomplished woman. Her honors included a Doctor of Humane Letters from New York University. However, when young, Sally was very much a tomboy. According to her brother Edward:

> *Miss Sally was not particularly good-looking. She had a rather flat figure, and when she was young she liked to play with the boys and lead them in pranks. However a prank of another kind was played on her. At home in Ringwood Manor there was a Cuban gentleman, Fernando Yznaga, who was always playing tricks on Sally. At a party at the Tuxedo Club where we were all skating, he played a trick on Sally, which made her furious. She had small feet and was very proud of them, as she had no other beauty. It was the custom, those days, for everyone to put their shoes outside their bedroom doors to have them cleaned. When Sally had gone to bed, Fernando took a large pair of men's shoes and put them beside Sally's dainty shoes, outside her door. Everyone, of course, saw the shoes there, as her room was right at the head of the main stairs. She was furious with Fernando, but she liked flattery and attention so much that she soon forgave him.*

Miss Sally may not have been a beauty, but she had infectious high spirits and was quick-witted and outspoken. Sally was a good organizer and lived up to Peter Cooper's assessment of her managerial skills. Later in life, she was known for her able management of the Forges and Manor, as well as the Hewitt farm, on the thirty-three-thousand-acre Ringwood estate. She was the real boss, and in most cases, what she said was the final decision. Her bedroom was located over the back end of the large hall, next to the side entrance from the driveway.

Sarah Cooper Hewitt, "Miss Sally Dressed." *Courtesy of Ringwood Manor, Ringwood State Park.*

In his book *Ringwood Manor: The Home of the Hewitts*, Edward Ringwood recalled Miss Sally's peculiarities:

> *In those days there were no electric bells in the house, because Sally distrusted them, so when she wanted the maid she used to open the window and blow a loud blast on an English coaching horn, which could be heard all over the household and far down the valley. Even when bells were installed, she still preferred to use her coach horn. She hated the telephone and wouldn't allow one in the house. She conceded that the telephone had its uses, however, and had a cement out-building constructed for just the purpose of housing it.*

Miss Sally had a feisty personality and seemed to be at the head and front of everything at Ringwood, and she believed that she should be represented in a school system in which she was so vitally interested since it had so much to do with the children of her tenants and workmen. The votes overwhelmed the candidate Dr. John Dyneley Prince and made Sally Hewitt the first woman to hold an elective office in the state of New Jersey. She was a success in public office and paid for most of the school improvements and teacher's salaries out of her own pocket.

Sarah Hewitt, dressed for the Vanderbilt ball in 1883; her costume was copied by Worth from Sarah Bernhardt's character "Roxanne." *Courtesy of Cooper-Hewitt, National Design Museum, Smithsonian Institution / Art Resource, New York Cooper-Hewitt, National Design Museum, New York City, New York, United States.*

A fond collector of bric-a-brac, Miss Sally also had a sharp eye and the great talent for collecting the finest-quality drawings, particularly those from the eighteenth century, for the museum. In later years, when she had a large and imposing size, she chose to travel through museums in a wheelchair, pushed by her loyal butler Darnley. Being clever was one of her outstanding traits. A larger-than-life raconteur, in social occasions Miss Sally usually captivated her audience. She was a fountain of ideas, but she could be easily bored and domineering, a characteristic that Sally seemed to have inherited from her father. Possessing a strong personality, Miss Sally eventually dominated Miss Nelly, who was smaller, more feminine, softer of voice and more docile than her older sister.

Eleanor Garnier Hewitt

Eleanor, fondly nicknamed "Miss Nelly," was the last daughter born to Abram and Amelia Hewitt and always lived in Peter Cooper's old house at 9 Lexington Avenue. Such intimacy led to daily contact with her grandfather during her entire girlhood, and he cast his influence on her at an early age. This close relationship with Peter Cooper, mingled with her executive ability, also enabled her to become a guiding force in The Cooper Union Museum for the Arts of Decoration. She never took full credit and always acknowledged that significant contributions to the museum had been made by her mother, Amelia, and her sisters, Amy and Sally.

Of Sally, Peter Cooper said that she was "full of life and gaiety," while Nelly unquestionably pleased him "for her purposeful, orderly and executive talent." Nelly was blond and good-looking, but there was never even a hint of frivolity in her demeanor. Both in work and play, she was a great organizer, and along these lines, she was sympathetic to her father, Abram, and to a certain extent became his private secretary in connection with many of his most important projects. She invented a private system of stenography and became one of the earliest female typists in the country. Sally wrote about Nelly's close relationship with her father, "Once in a century has a daughter enjoyed such an intimate and inspiring association with one of the great men of his age during the years of his supreme activity."

Comments printed in the memoriam for Eleanor Garnier Hewitt, published in the sixty-sixth and sixty-seventh annual reports of The Cooper Union, attest to her fine qualities: "As a young girl, Eleanor was popular in general society. Nelly had a fine disposition and was most affectionate and generous. She was a beautiful dancer and frequently danced through a pair of slippers on a single night, yet the following morning, she was up and dressed early, pursuing a regular course of daily studies." Nelly's hands seemed never to be idle. She was a wizard with her needle, working on a beautiful piece of embroidery, and sketched constantly or made designs in a book that never left her side.

Eleanor possessed a vital and athletically driven personality. She was a remarkable athlete, having been trained with her three brothers in the private gymnasium installed by Peter Cooper behind their home at 9 Lexington Avenue. The sisters were among the pioneers as sportswomen in riding, hunting and skating, and they loved horses and dogs and claimed to have imported the first game of lawn tennis to America from England. Whether this fact is truth or fiction, by 1885, the new sport of lawn tennis had become popular. Hundreds of tennis clubs sprang up throughout the city, especially in Brooklyn, where many acres in Prospect Park were set aside for the sport. People also went to the North Meadows in Central Park for lawn tennis, croquet and picnics. By 1886, cycling was fast taking over the roadways in Central Park and Riverside Drive. In 1894, women found new freedom wearing clothing innovated by Amelia Bloomer, who introduced women to a form of pants called bloomers. From then on, there was no holding women back, and they cycled away into the awakening of the suffragist movement.

At Ringwood Manor, Eleanor shot, rowed, canoed, sailed, swam and climbed mountains. She possessed certain bravado, and her physical strength and courage were rare in women at the time. Miss Nelly always directed the development of the gardens at Ringwood, though her mother from the beginning also shared a great deal of influence. In creating the Ringwood gardens, Miss Nelly referenced the notations made in her little leather travel diaries about legendary gardens in Europe. She especially took charge of the planting of the fruit trees. Whatever she turned her enthusiasm to, she undertook with thoroughness, whether it was gardening or devising a system of classifying the objects in the museum for the most convenient use.

Miss Nelly was a primary force in the formation of the museum, and it was her enthusiasm for books dealing with the arts of decoration that inspired the council to purchase the Leon Decloux Collection of illustrated books by the greatest "Maitres Ornemenists" of the eighteenth century. The collection was so well known in Paris that its ownership converted The Cooper Union Museum for the Arts of Decoration into a museum of high educational value. At Ringwood, she conducted lessons in the arts and authored a booklet entitled *The Making of a Modern Museum*, which she delivered as a speech of the same name at a meeting of the Wednesday Afternoon Club in 1919. Miss Nelly was given many gifts to exploit her talents, and no task was too great for her capable hands. She devoted her life to various interests, particularly the arts, associated with The Cooper Union, where she was secretary of the Ladies' Advisory Council of The Cooper Union Cooking School and the Free Library.

TRAVELS WITH DARNLEY

Collectively, the sisters shared a unique bond and traveled frequently to Europe to acquire rare and unique decorative objects and to satisfy their craving for

The Hewitt sisters—Amy, Sarah and Eleanor—on one of their many trips abroad. *Courtesy of Cooper-Hewitt, National Design Museum, Smithsonian Institution / Art Resource, New York Cooper-Hewitt, National Design Museum, New York City, New York, United States.*

cultural enlightenment. Like her sister, Miss Nelly had a natural talent, a "good eye," in the collector's sense, and she and Sally bought all manner of textiles and laces, drawings, prints and decorative objects. They instinctively knew quality, and to their benefit, they had the influence of their father Abram's fine French taste for the decorative arts. Both ladies spoke flawless French and had an impressive knowledge of French literature and the historical past.

On their Grand Tour, they customarily traveled every summer and went on expeditions of discovery and collecting in France, Italy and Switzerland. Before Amy married Dr. James O. Green, she also accompanied her sisters on these trips. On each journey, the sisters were accompanied by their loyal butler Darnley—not a lady's maid, as was the custom of many fashionable women in the Victorian era, but more of a polite bodyguard, butler, waiter and courier. A large, imposing man, Darnley had once been batman to Lord Roberts of Kandahar and was unflappable. He was one of the few men the Hewitt sisters trusted, as they both had an uncanny distrust of men. In the bloom of their youth, both sisters were quite attractive, and there is evidence that they had had several opportunities to marry but preferred to make careers for themselves. If they had married, their freedom to travel and pursue their museum goals would certainly have been substantially limited, and the control of their finances would most likely have been handled by their husbands. No doubt those minor considerations may have factored into the sisters' desire to remain single, but their main objective, which they never lost sight of, was to have full control of their museum activities.

ON THE HIGH SEAS

Miss Sally in particular suspected all men except her butler. Miss Nelly, on the other hand, feared more the natural forces of travel. On transatlantic crossings, she would wear two padded Chinese costumes, one over the other, mistakenly believing that she would keep warm if she found herself in the icy ocean.

Darnley was an invaluable addition to their entourage, and in his role as traveling companion, he buffered the difficulties of Victorian travel. In the role of maid, he often served the sisters their meals in the suite of the hotel in each city where they were staying—they had become somewhat reclusive and did not like the tedium of hotel dining rooms.

Nelly and Sally regularly traveled to Europe on the *Mauretania*, the only ship they would use or trust for their sea journey. It belonged to the Cunard Line, and the Hewitt family knew the Cunards.

The sisters were fortunate travelers to have at their disposal contacts with influential people who could make their journey more pleasurable. They also received letters of introduction from acquaintances in their social circle.

In preparation for one of their European trips, a friendly letter of introduction dated May 27, 1922, from Mr. Louis R. Metcalf provided a referral as follows:

My dear Miss Hewitt:

I hope that these lines find you well and delighted with your surroundings. What a splendid trip you are going to have! Would that I could suddenly come across you in the Piazza delle Erbe, or the Theatre d'Orange! I could not send my article on the etchings of Tiepolo to the steamer, as it was still in the press. As it is, the American public is still to wait with bated breath for its appearance! Such is the age of strikes! To Monsieur Verazi I wrote a lengthy epistle, which I enjoyed immensely, for it enabled me to tell him all I knew about the Misses Hewitt. I feel sure that he has already put his house in order and reread Lady Dieke and that he is watching for your arrival. Do try to stop at Bordereux and look him up. You will find him well posted on the Musee des Arts Decoratif, and the monument of Peter Cooper. 19 rue de Grassi is his address. I look forward with such pleasure and gratitude to the happy hours you have allowed me to spend at 9 Lexington Ave!

Believe me, with great regards to Miss Hewitt and all good wishes for your summer.

Sincerely yours,

Louis R. Metcalf

FASHIONABLE WOMEN

Along with their mother, Amelia, and their sister Amy, Nelly and Sally made frequent visits to Paris to purchase their fashionable gowns, like other women of their social class. Adapting the penchant for the "French taste," they frequented the celebrated haute couture houses of Paris, notably the House of Worth and sometimes Paquin. Although the Hewitt sisters may have patronized other couture salons, most of their gowns bore the Worth label. The House of Worth was the first couture salon in Paris. It set the standard for the couture and specialized in creating one-of-a-kind made-to-measure wardrobe ensembles and extravagant gowns for women of discerning taste and wealth.

Charles Frederick Worth, the eminent designer, was a self-made guru of fashion, and visiting his couture house was an intimidating experience. For one thing, he fancied himself an artist of fashion and wore a beret and artist's smock. Mr. Worth was a colorful character, a self-described dictator of fashion, and he ruled over most of his clients with strong hand. Not so with the Hewitt sisters, who insisted that their gowns be both "au currant" and practical. They found that the gowns were at least two years ahead of the fashions in New York, and so they would put the dresses away until they were not so conspicuous for being outré. One curious consideration for the purchase of a couture dress concerned a stepladder. When the Hewitt sisters were fitted, they insisted that a stepladder be provided so that they could test out the garments they would be wearing as they scaled the stacks and clambered about in the library of their museum.

In the book *The Opulent Era*, author Elizabeth Ann Coleman recounted that the House of Worth was known for its exquisite if not elaborate use of bold patterns, rich silks and damasks in vibrant colors. These materials particularly suited the Hewitt sisters' interest in textiles because they favored adaptations of historic textiles. Worth was an able supplier, particularly adaptations of eighteenth-century women's riding outfits, derived from the cut of a man's body coat. Miss Nelly had a penchant for wearing menswear-inspired garments in her daily wardrobe, as well as equestrian-inspired garments for sporting activities. To accommodate her preferences, "Worth even went as far as to make women's jackets from the elaborately decorated men's dress coats of a century earlier. Such pieces were literally made-to-order for Miss Nelly. The mannish clothes she affected had to be of the finest fabrics; for the Hewitt women, textiles were their passion."

Their friend, the art dealer Germain Seligman, recalled that as the Hewitt sisters grew older, "They retained the patterns of their youth, and the sumptuous materials of their gowns were still fashioned in the old modes as were their hats!" And Allyn Cox noted, "In green and purple patterns, they were quite a sight!"

The Hewitt sisters lived exactly as they wished, without regard for fashion or convention. They were individualists in the best sense of the word, and despite their old New York habits, their paramount concern and passion remained deeply rooted in acquiring textiles and decorative arts for The Cooper Union Museum.

THE TRAVEL DIARIES

The Hewitt sisters became "petite" travel journalists, and during their trips abroad, they briefly documented the gardens, sanctuaries and marvels of Europe. As well-bred young women of the era, they had instruction in drawing, music and poetry and were equally capable of making notations about the places they visited. With skills of this modest nature, Nelly and Sally filled small pocket-sized maroon leather diaries with sketches of buildings, gardens, façades and landscapes that were often accompanied by notations written in English or French. Many of the inscriptions were handwritten in soft lead pencil, but there is no telling which of the sisters actually wrote or executed the charming sketches, as none of the drawings are signed. A secretary was also engaged to type many of their comments, perhaps in the country they were visiting or as summaries when the sisters returned from their travels. The small pages containing dates, places, gardens and descriptions illustrate that the sisters were skilled observers and narrators of historic places. One of the typed descriptions of a visit to Como includes these abbreviations exactly as written:

> *Como-Villa d'Este, only old garden keeping fragment orig arch, at Cernobbio mile or two from Como. Built in 1527 by Car. Gallio 1816. Caroline Brunswich, who called Este, turned it into great structure Empire style. Now fashionable hotel ground anglicized but main lines of Renaissance Garden exist. Bosco of Villa d'Este one of the most enchanting bits of Sylvan Gardening in Italy. Grove of old plane trees water gate enchanting.*

The Hewitt sisters' reputation as procurers of the decorative objects for the museum was aided by the advantage of having both social and business connections. Letters and tactful information were forthcoming on a regular basis. In a letter dated June 23, 1924, an architect named Henry Milliken, at 4 East Thirty-ninth Street, New York, wrote:

> *My dear Miss Hewitt,*

> *The monument of which I spoke is apparently a small wall monument at Rosny-sur-Seine. The photographer, who would have this card and who you will also find very valuable on documents and decorative arts, is Mr. Ollivier, No. 6 rue de Seine, Paris. I am writing to him today to procure this, if he has not already got it, and have it ready for you.*

> *Sincerely,*

> *Henry Milliken*

The Hewitt sisters' little travel missives were miniature treasure-troves of pertinent travel data and also served as handy references of sightseeing information, which they shared with their friends. In a letter to a woman addressed merely as Edith, Nelly wrote, "Sevres, be sure to see ceramic museum, upstairs particularly. Lovely place for tea at Pavillon Bleu at Bellevue where Mme de Pompadour's chateau was, then further uphill through the marvelous Allee to Meudon, see view from terrasse, at farther end pretty garden and orangerie & remains of 17th cent chateau."

One of the sisters—perhaps it was Eleanor because she was fluent in French like her sister—wrote in one of the tiny leather diaries an observation about a doll museum and described the dolls' attire as perfect examples of national costumes in every detail.

MORE THAN MEETS THE EYE

It is often believed that money is all that one needs to assemble an art collection, but the Hewitt sisters' love of the decorative arts, tact, persistence and dedication were the qualities that created The Cooper Union Museum for the Art of Decoration. "The salient point," Eleanor Hewitt insisted, "is that objects are there for use, to be worked from, and, if so desired, to be removed from their positions and placed in any light." The collections eventually went on to inspire a new heightened awareness of the decorative arts not only in New York but also throughout the nation. The Smithsonian, Cooper-Hewitt National Design Museum is still a working museum imbued with the spirit of the Cooper and Hewitt families, and it is the only museum in the nation devoted exclusively to historic and contemporary design, providing students, designers and the general public with new ways to appreciate both the aesthetics and function of design. The Smithsonian, Cooper-Hewitt National Design Museum, housed in the landmark Andrew Carnegie Mansion, is the repository of one of the great design collections of the western world.

THE LADIES ORCHESTRA

Philanthropy and charity, examples set by their father, Abram Hewitt, and their grandfather, Peter Cooper, were inherited principles in the Hewitt sisters' upbringing. Although the sisters were occupied in serious pursuits, principally The Cooper Union Museum for the Arts of Decoration, they had other diversions that engaged their talents and spirit of philanthropy. Social activities in old New York, parties, balls and diverse entertainments occupied a good deal of their private time, but true to their calling, the Hewitt sisters seemed to have always had a sense of duty to contribute to the welfare of society.

One of the most spirited ideas conceived by the Hewitt sisters was the creation of the Ladies Amateur Orchestra, the first and only one of its kind in New York City and perhaps also in the United States. It is suggested that Lady Folkstone's orchestra in England may have inspired the concept of the Hewitt sisters' orchestra, for Miss Sally and Miss Nelly had traveled abroad extensively. During one of their European trips, they were invited to the rehearsal of a ladies orchestra in London under the management and patronage of Lady Folkstone. Her orchestra had become a brilliant feature of London society, and the members were titled women and daughters of aristocratic families.

Inspired by this concept, the Hewitt sisters' orchestra primarily adapted the upper-class model set in England. The orchestra would consist of talented young women culled from the families of old New York who came from diverse social backgrounds, albeit wealthy ones.

Nelly and Sally were young women of considerable musical talent and ambition, but the moving spirit of the Ladies Amateur Orchestra is attributed to Miss Sally, who had inherited much of her father's genius for organization and a love of music and the arts. The obstacles that would have deterred most enthusiasts from such an undertaking did not deter Miss Sally. Au contraire, she felt convinced that there was plenty of musical talent among New York society girls that would, if brought together and properly trained and directed, have results just as credible as those achieved by the London prototypes.

Miss Sally would prove to be an excellent taskmaster for the orchestra undertaking. Music was her passion, and almost since she was old enough to talk, she had played the violin. When she grew up, she desired to train her talent under the discipline of a regular orchestra and persuaded her teacher, Herr Reinhard Schmelz, to help organize an orchestra among his lady pupils. Miss Sally used all her own influence to arouse interest in the orchestra and soon found many congenial friends with the same wish. Eventually, the sisters eliminated the word "Amateur" from the title and simply called their enterprise the Ladies Orchestra.

Miss Nelly was also an excellent musician in her own right and had great musical ability. She not only played the viola well but also played the violin, the harp, the guitar and the piano. One can only assume that the brainy young women had purpose in their mind when they set about to form all-girl orchestra. At first, it appeared that the orchestra's intent was merely to entertain their friends at lively socials at their father's mansion, the old Peter Cooper home on Lexington Avenue. However, their raison d'être later became more magnanimous as the orchestra became increasingly in demand to perform for benefit events.

The formation of the orchestra was not in any way a frivolous contrivance but was instead regarded as a serious undertaking. From the beginning, it was arranged that candidates for admission must pass a musical examination, as well as pay a membership fee, before they could get the favorable consideration of the officers. This step was taken in order to ensure that members should have sufficient ability to make the work of the orchestra satisfactory from a musical point of view. And so, strict rules for membership were set forth to engage only those young women who could comply with the following:

> *The Ladies Orchestra Society will have its meetings the second week in November, 1885, to the second week in May 1886. It will be composed entirely of ladies, who must be amateurs, and play upon violins, violas, violoncellos, and double basses.*
>
> *The Society will be conducted by Herr Reinhard Schmelz a professional leader, who will have full power to assign members their parts, and change their positions in the orchestra.*
>
> *Rehearsals will take place every Saturday, from 11 a.m. to 1 p.m.*
>
> *A fine of fifteen cents will be imposed every time a member is absent or late or leaves before it closes. Members are particularly requested to come fifteen minutes before 11 o'clock, in order to tune their instruments in advance so that the rehearsals may commence promptly and without confusion.*
>
> *The annual dues will be Five Dollars, payable the last Saturday in November. This money will be used to buy music for the Society.*
>
> *All music shall belong to the Society, and shall be given up by members in case of resignation.*
>
> *Members shall be responsible for their music, and must replace it if lost or damaged.*
>
> *Members are expected to practice their parts without fail between the rehearsals.*
>
> *Members are requested to give early notice to the Secretary if they are obliged to be absent from a rehearsal.*
>
> *Persons wishing to become members must apply to one of the officers of the Society. An examination for musical proficiency will be required.*

As an after note, the rules further added the following warning: "During the intervals of playing members are earnestly requested not to indulge in conversation, or in any way interrupt the explanations and instructions of the leader." The rules were signed by Sarah Cooper Hewitt, president; Frances Johnston, treasurer; and Eleanor Garnier Hewitt, secretary.

In 1885, the ambitious Ladies Orchestra was officially established, and one Saturday morning, thirty-two members, young women of prominent social position in old New York, met for its first rehearsal in the music room of the Hewitt house. The members of the orchestra were among the best-known belles of New York society and included Miss Remsen, viola, the daughter of Robert G. Remsen of Fifth Avenue and one of a large family of unusually clever girls. Miss Knox and Mrs. Schenck, both members of old Knickerbocker families, were two of the girls who also played the viola, while Miss Drexel, one of the lovely daughters of the prominent banker Joseph Drexel, was the harpist of the orchestra. Indeed, the whole Drexel family was musical, Mr. Drexel being a notable violoncellist and Mrs. Drexel a pianist. Mrs. Stanford White, wife of the famed architect, played the bass fiddle. With one exception, Miss Emmet, one of the second violinists, was one of the most accomplished members of the orchestra. The violin she played is said to be two centuries old and is a family heirloom. Adding professional status to the orchestra, their leader and music director Herr Reinhard Schmelz was a musician of the first rank and had been identified with many of the best musical events in the city.

On that Saturday morning, with thirty-two members coming together with such diverse personalities and novice talents, Herr Schmelz had no idea how challenging a task it would be to rally the amateur talents available to him into a cohesive orchestra.

For the first hour of rehearsal, as would be expected of the initial trials, Herr Schmelz found that the cacophony of sound was miles away from what he expected. The girls were obviously nervous; they had never played to the baton before, and somehow the classical little etude they rehearsed would not go right. Finally, in despair, a Waltenfel waltz was tried, and all at once a sweet melody came forth.

The Ladies Orchestra members pressed on with faith in their hearts and a determination to succeed. All during the winter, the members of the orchestra were steadfast and serious. Music, as these young ladies cultivated it, was no idle pastime. They gathered faithfully once a week at Mayor Hewitt's house and played together, and each girl practiced diligently at home.

The rules set forth for membership illustrated the serious nature of their commitment. During the summer, they were of course separated, but they met again in the fall, and every week they rehearsed with the zeal and diligence of paid professionals. Consequently, they formed an orchestra noted for its perfection of technique, time and expression. These thirty-two girls played some of the most difficult classical selections, and the best musicians gave them only praise for their own excellence. Fortified with such recommendations, the orchestra had courage to perform at a private reception.

As the members of the orchestra were society's own belles, the reviews in the press recorded their first private performance. The *Herald Tribune* headline for February 17, 1888, announced, "Pretty Girls with Violins," followed by the text, "The orchestra gave a musicale at the Hewitt mansion and some four hundred of their personal friends came to hear them." The newspaper account continued in a favorable vein, noting, "Thirty-two charming girls all dressed to perfection in laces and silk, sitting grouped in a magnificent apartment and playing classical music in perfect harmony, was the sight that met the eyes of the guests yesterday afternoon."

The newspaper article took full advantage of the event and further described, "The guests were ushered into a great marble hallway and left their wraps in the library. Mrs. Hewitt and her daughters received the guests at the head of the broad marble stairway. They were then ushered into the drawing room on the second floor, which together with the music room and hall was decorated with cut flowers from the Ringwood conservatory. The program under the direction of Herr Reinhard Schmelz began with the following programme, printed on pink tinted cards, with the names of the members of the orchestra and their respective instruments printed on the reverse side."

A newspaper account in the *New York Sun* on February 17, 1888, also praised the performance: "The program in many ways was well carried out and the overture to the 'Magic Flute,' by Mozart, opened the program. A Turkish March from the 'Ruins of Athens' by Beethoven and Massenet's 'La Dernier Sommeil de la Vierge' was performed with much spirit and the same could be said for many of the other pieces."

These accolades did not go to the orchestra member's heads. They continued to hone their skills. After several other musicales in which the Ladies Orchestra performed for private audiences, they had proved their professionalism and were proficient enough for a public event.

The Ladies Orchestra was ready. So, too, was the press ready to record the unique performance of New York's society belles. The *Herald's* headline story "Young Ladies of New York About to Give Public Concerts" reported that "the Ladies Amateur Orchestra will play for the first time in public at charity matinees arranged for February 23 and 24 at the Lyceum Theatre."

The world of society turned out en masse for the Ladies Orchestra, and long before 2:30 p.m., Fourth Avenue was well lined with carriages for some blocks up and down. The musical entertainment was for the benefit of the Skin and Cancer Hospital and the Sheltering Arms, and the audience packed the Lyceum Theatre to the doors.

The *Herald* article continued:

> *When the curtain rose a great gasp of delighted echoed throughout the Lyceum. It revealed a pastoral woodland scene with the ladies of the orchestra standing on the stage instead of sitting before their music racks. Only Miss Pillsbury, Miss Parker and Miss Arnold, who played the cellos, and Mrs. Drexel, who played the harp were seated.*
>
> *As they stood and sat in graceful poses all the young women wore demi-toilets, a simple white faille Francaise gown with a light blue sash across their right shoulder tied in a graceful bow at the side. The sash was held in place by a brooch and some of these brooches blazed with diamonds, and others were of cut steel. Seen at a distance all had the same dazzling effect. This was one of the most charming sights revealed on the public stage in old New York. Society had never seen its "pets" in such a role before and was almost astonished when the curtains parted.*
>
> *There was a burst of spontaneous, warm applause, such as was seldom heard at an amateur affair. The thirty earnest maidens, lovely and blushing with enthusiasm appeared confident and ready to perform. Some players smiled, much pleased, while others too nervous even to smile stood watching the baton of their leader, Herr Schmelz. Tension mounted in the hearts of the ladies but, not to disappoint the assembled guests, they rose to the occasion. Like the professionals they had become Maestro Schmelz engaged the Ladies Orchestra in musical symmetry and introduced the program with Mozart's overture to the Magic Flute.*
>
> *Then the orchestra played the Bach-Wilhelmj air on the G string, Max Bruch's introduction to "Loreley" and familiar Hungarian Dances by Brahms. In response to the audience's mounted applause and enthusiasm they played as an encore the "Turkish March" from Beethoven's "Ruins of Athens." Their conductor was evidently a man of considerable modesty, for he refused to look at the audience or to accept for himself any of the applause bestowed upon the work of his pupils. The very existence of the Ladies Orchestra and this successful public performance strongly rebuked the cynics who were constantly growling about the flippancy of fashionable society.*

After such a public triumph with a charitable purpose, the orchestra's reputation for excellence brought other invitations to perform. And so they rested on their laurels and praise and continued to perform on numerous other occasions for private and public audiences, garnering funds for charitable causes.

INVITATION TO PERFORM FOR WOMAN'S SUFFRAGE

Despite their thrust into the public arena and publicity garnered by their Ladies Orchestra, when it came to politics, the Hewitt women remained rather unsophisticated and unsympathetic toward supporting a major cause that would benefit women. Like many other ladies of their social class, they had negative views on political topics, particularly on the subject of woman's suffrage.

It is disappointing that the Hewitt sisters, who were world travelers and had championed the founding of The Cooper Union Museum for the Arts of Decoration, did not endorse the right to vote. When Susan B. Anthony asked Sally if the orchestra would lead the program at the fortieth anniversary of the International Council of the Woman Suffrage Association, there is no record of Miss Sally's acceptance.

The Hewitt sisters' political sentiments were also made clear when, six years later, Eleanor Garnier Hewitt served as treasurer of the New York Association, which was opposed to the extension of suffrage to women. Finding the exercise of the vote, among other things, unjust and cruel, this organization looked on suffrage "not as a right to be enjoyed, but as a duty to be performed." As a matter of fact, the Hewitt sisters and their mother felt that their husbands and brothers were best prepared to make decisions on their behalf. Such was the attitude of many women of the upper-class ranks of society who opposed the vote. However, not all opposing women were silent. Several prominent antisuffrage women were active in social welfare work and philanthropy; others were successful authors and university professors.

CONCLUSION

The Hewitt sisters left a legacy that raised the Cooper-Hewitt dynasty of New York into the halls of historical reverence. Their pioneering accomplishment as museum curators was a calling for which they seemed destined to fulfill from the start of Peter Cooper's vision and their father Abram Steven Hewitt's encouragement.

At a time when most women remained comfortable in their role as society belles, the Hewitt sisters were shrewd women who mastered their destinies and places in history as the founders of The Cooper Union Museum for the Arts of Decoration. They serve as an inspiration for women today who are determined to succeed in a world of impossible dreams.

At the age of sixty, Miss Nelly died suddenly of bronchitis at Ringwood Manor, and with her went the good humor, enthusiasm and profound organizing instincts that benefited the museum's development. Her funeral was held at Calvary Church near Gramercy Park, and Mr. J. Pierpont Morgan, the son of her early benefactor, was one of the honorary pallbearers. Six years later, Miss Sally's funeral was held at the same church. Posthumously, Nelly shared one honor with her sister. In 1926, the Architectural League of New York jointly awarded them a "special medal," designed by their old friend Daniel Chester French, for their distinguished service to the allied art.

An editorial in the *New York Times* the day after Miss Sally's death noted, "A lady of the Old School, she belonged to 'the 400,' but she was not under the restraint of its social precedents. She and her sister made their own. They had also made a Modern Museum."

Epilogue

After the death of Abram Hewitt, his wife, Amelia, willed at her death in 1912 the Ringwood properties to her two unmarried daughters, Sarah Cooper and Eleanor Garnier Hewitt. After the daughters' deaths, the Forges and Manor of Ringwood were willed to Erskine Hewitt, a bachelor, who had no desire to keep up the big house and lived in a cottage on one of the Cupsaw lakes. In 1936, he deeded the properties—Ringwood Manor, as the house is called, and several hundred acres—to the State of New Jersey and stipulated that the land be maintained as a state park.

As Edward Ringwood recalled, "Ringwood house was never the same to me after my mother's death. Life seemed to have gone out of the place, and I no longer cared to visit it. To me it was the home of the family, full of all kinds of family association. It seems suitable to me that no other family will ever live there. It was a most wonderful home, where everything that could make for the pleasure and recreation of a growing family took place, as that kind of life has probably disappeared forever from the American scene."

Bibliography

Books

Abell, Arthur M. *Talks with Great Composers*. Germany: G.E. Schroeder-Verlag, 1964.

Adams, Henry B. *The Education of Henry Adams*. Boston, MA: self-published, 1907. Reprint, Boston, MA: Harcourt, 1918.

Beckert, Sven. *The Moneyed Metropolis*. New York: Cambridge University Press, 2001.

"The Biography of Peter Cooper, Written by Nathan C. Walker in the Dictionary of Unitarian Universalist Biography." On-line resource, Unitarian Universalist History & Heritage Society, New York.

The Bowery Boys, New York City History, theboweryboys.blogspot.com.

Brown, William H. *The History of the First Locomotives in America*. New York: D. Appleton and Company, 1874.

Coleman, Elizabeth Ann. *The Opulent Era*. New York: Thames and Hudson Inc., 1989.

Cottrell, Alden T. *The Story of Ringwood Manor*. Ringwood, NJ: North Jersey Highlands Historical Society, 1988.

Ellis, Edward Robb. *The Epic of New York City*. New York: Coward-McCann, 1966. Reprint, New York: Kodansha USA, 1997.

Grafton, John. *New York in the Nineteenth Century*. New York: Dover Publications Inc., 1977 and 1980.

Hellman, Geoffrey T. "A Reporter at Large, No. 9 Lexington Avenue." *New Yorker*, October 29, 1938, 58–65.

Heusser, Albert H. *The Forgotten General*. Reprint, New Brunswick, NJ: Rutgers University Press, 1966. Originally published in 1928.

Hewitt, Edward Ringwood. *Ringwood Manor: The Home of the Hewitts*. Trenton, NJ: Trenton Printing Company, 1946.

———. *Those Were the Days: Tales of a Long Life*. New York: Duell, Sloan and Pearce, 1943.

Hewitt, Eleanor Garnier. *The Making of a Modern Museum*. Booklet written for the Wednesday Afternoon Club, New York, 1919.

Hewitt, Erskine. *Forges and Manor of Ringwood*. Booklet. New Jersey, 1935.

History of Morris County, New Jersey. Vol. 2. New York: Lewis Publishing Company, 1914.

Lewis, Alfred Allan. *Ladies and Not-So-Gentle Women*. New York, Penguin Putnam Inc., 2000.

Lynes, Russell. *More than Meets the Eye: The History of the Collections of Cooper-Hewitt Museum, the Smithsonian Institution's National Museum of Design*. Washington, D.C.: Smithsonian, 1981.

Morris, Lloyd. *Incredible New York*. New York: Random House, 1951.

Nevins, Allan. *Abram S. Hewitt with Some Account of Peter Cooper*. New York: Harper & Brothers, 1935. Reprint, New York: Octagon Books, 1967.

Wests, Louis P. "Ringwood's 50th Anniversary." *Ringwood Review* 2, no. 2 (1993). Ringwood, New Jeresey, Ringwood Public Library: "I Remember Ringwood" Series.

Wyman, Carolyn. *JELL-O, a Biography: The History and Mystery of "America's Most Famous Dessert."* New York: Harvest/Harcourt Paperback, 2001.

RESEARCH

All Souls Unitarian Church Archives, New York City, New York.

Haverstraw King's Daughters Public Library, Garnerville, New York.

Haverstraw Library, Village Branch, Haverstraw, New York.

The Hewitt sisters' papers, located at The Cooper Union Library, New York City, New York.

Huguenot Society of America, New York City, New York.

Johnson, Marilynn A. "John Hewitt, Cabinetmaker." *Winterthur Portfolio* 4 (1968): 185–205. Published by the University of Chicago Press (Printed Book & Periodical Collection, Winterthur Museum, Gardens & Library).

The Library of the General Society of Mechanics & Tradesmen of the City of New York.

Morgan Library & Museum, New York City, New York.

Museum of the City of New York.

New Jersey Historical Society, Newark, New Jersey.

New York Historical Society, New York City, New York.

Peter Cooper's papers, located in the Special Section Division of The Cooper Union Library.

Ringwood Manor, Ringwood State Park, Ringwood, New Jersey.

Ringwood Public Library, Ringwood, New Jersey.

Smithsonian, Cooper-Hewitt National Design Museum Library, New York City, New York.

South of the Mountain 14, no. 3 (July–September 1970). Published by the Historical Society of Rockland County, New City, New York.

Toledo-Lucas County Public Library, Toledo, Ohio.

Tuxedo Park historian Chris Sonne.

Tuxedo Park Public Library, Tuxedo Park, New York.

NEWSPAPERS

Detroit Evening News, *Ann Arbor Argus*. "Governor Ashley's Daughter's Wedding." September 9, 1892.

Herald Tribune. "Pretty Girls with Violins." February 17, 1888.

———. "Young Ladies About to Give Public Concerts." February 17, 1888.

New York Daily Times. "To Science and Art." January 21, 1858.

New York Sun. "The Program in Many Ways Was Well Carried Out." February 17, 1888.

New York Times. "Clever Character Acting." April 6, 1899.

———. "Cooper Union's Crowning Glory, Its Museum of Decorative Arts." May 29, 1907.

———. "Great Throng at Church." June 11, 1924.

———. "*Makers of the Glue Trade*." April 7, 1883.

————. "Prince Viggo Weds an American Girl, Notable Gathering of Society as Miss Green Becomes Danish Nobleman's Bride." June 11, 1924.

————. "Yesterday's Weddings." November 16, 1886.

LANDMARKS

The Cooper Union for the Advancement of Science and Art.
51 Astor Place, New York, NY 10003.

The Cooper Union Library.
7 East Seventh Street, New York, NY 10003.

The General Society of Mechanics & Tradesmen of the City of New York and the Huguenot Society of America.
20 West Forty-fourth Street, New York, NY 10036.

The Peter Cooper House at 9 Lexington Avenue was demolished in the 1940s.

Ringwood Manor, a National Historic Landmark, Ringwood State Park.
1304 Sloatsburg Road, Ringwood, NJ 07456.

The Smithsonian, Cooper-Hewitt National Design Museum.
2 East Ninety-first Street, New York, NY 10128-8330.

About the Author

Polly Guérin is a former adjunct professor at the Fashion Institute of Technology in New York and the author of four college textbooks and two video productions. Her features on the decorative arts, antiques, collectibles and design have appeared in *Art & Antiques* magazine. She also writes on fashion and Art Deco and is currently the author of four blogs: pollytalkfromnewyork; menremarkablevisionaries; womendeterminedtosucceed and poetryfromtheheartbypollyguerin.

Ms. Guérin counts among her professional memberships—and is a board member of—the Art Deco Society of New York (ADSNY), the American Revolutionary Round Table (ARRT) and the Giulio Gari Foundation. She is also a member of the Victorian Society, Metro Chapter.

Visit us at
www.historypress.net